SNOOP DOGG'S TREATS to EAT

SNOOP DOGG'S TREATS to EAT

55 RECIPES FOR BAKING WITH (OR WITHOUT) WEED

PHOTOGRAPHY BY
ANTONIS ACHILLEOS

CHRONICLE BOOKS
SAN FRANCISCO

INTRODUCTION BY SNOOP 8

CHAPTER 1
BASICS [12]

CHAPTER 2
COOKIES [28]

CHAPTER 3
BROWNIES, BLONDIES, AND MUFFINS [52]

CHAPTER 4
CAKES, PIES, AND PUDDINGS [78]

CHAPTER 5

WAKE AND BAKES [102]

CHAPTER 6

CANDIES, SNACKS, AND SAVORIES [122]

CHAPTER 7

DRINKS [150]

INDEX 170

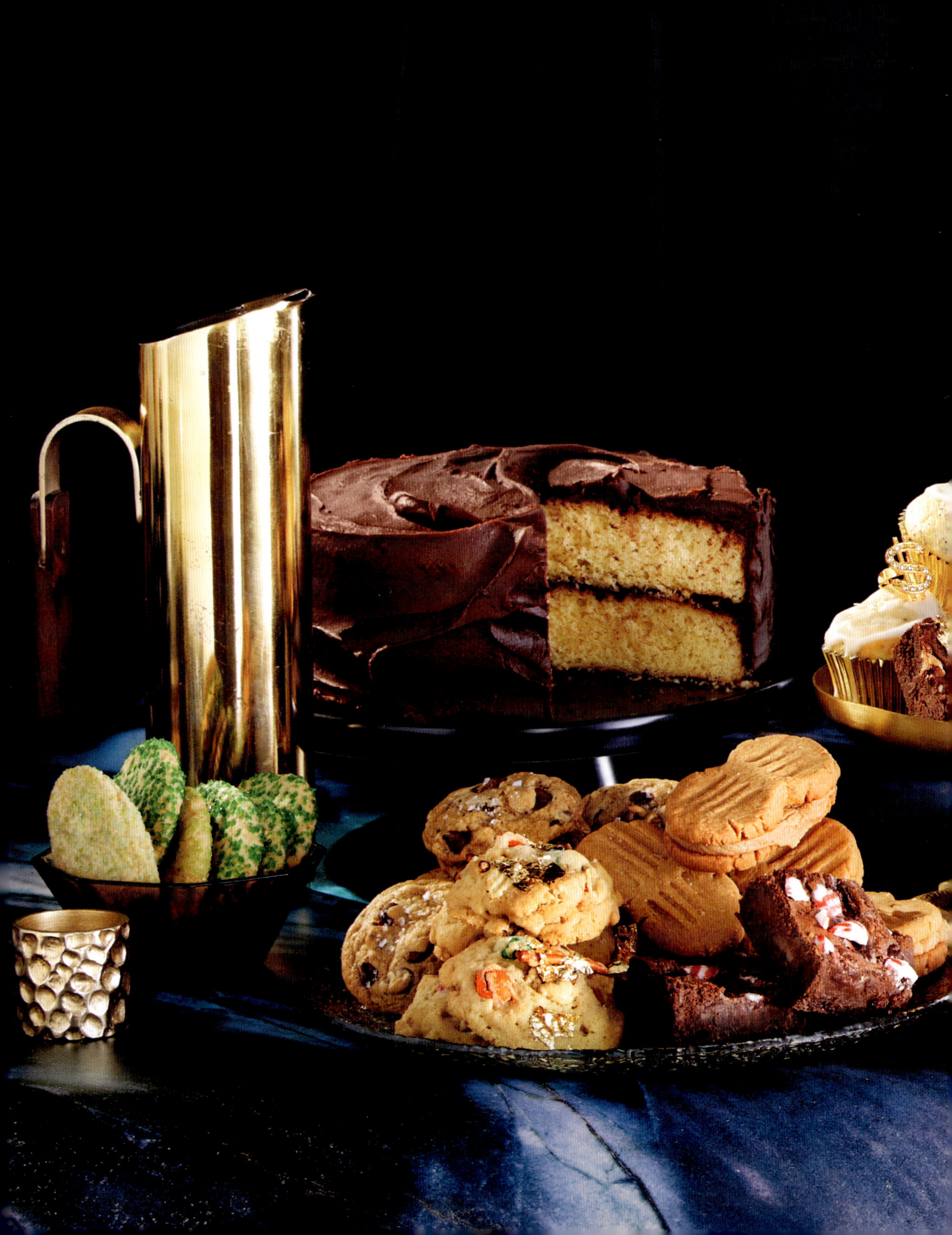

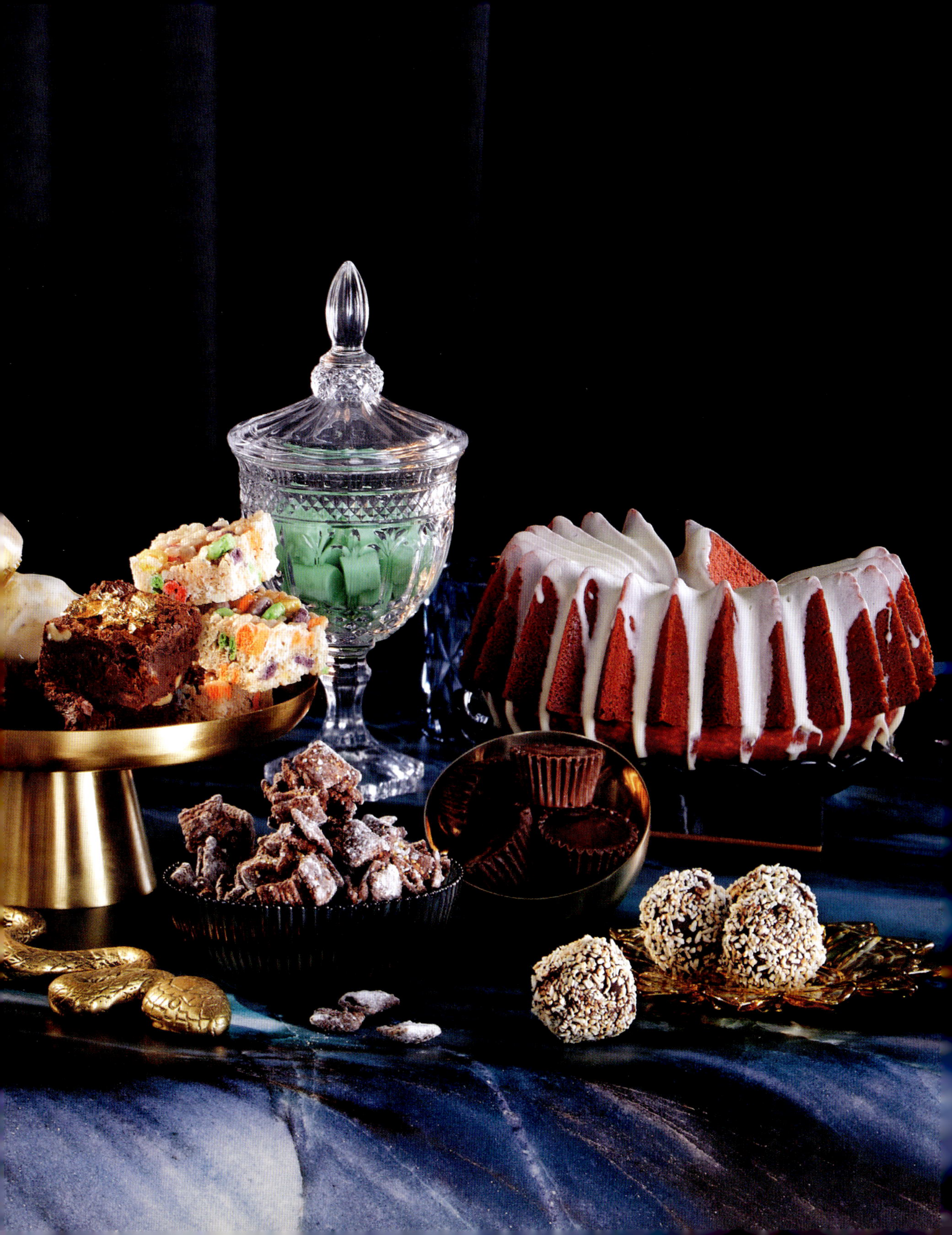

INTRODUCTION

SMOKE WEED EVERY DAY & BAKE WITH THE BOSS OF THE CHRONIC

Yo, what up my fellow flavor chasers and cannabis creators: You already know what time it is, and I'm here to welcome you to a whole new level of culinary creativity. This ain't your grandma's baking book (unless your grandma was rolling joints and dough at the same time). This here is HIGH cuisine, baby . . .

See, I've been around the world and I've tasted the finest treats and puffed the loudest blunts—but there is something magical about that homemade magic. Whether it's brownies that hit like a classic G-funk baseline or cookies that have you floatin' like you just dropped your first album, this book has all the goodies for your perfect culinary vibe.

Weed brings folks together. I'll never forget smoking my first blunt with Tupac. It sparked a friendship that ran deep. These platinum recipes are gonna get you cooking from mornin' to night. We gotcha covered with wake-and-bakes like my Bud-dermilk Pancakes with Stoner Syrup (page 110) to late-night cocktails like my classic Jacked-Up Gin 'n'

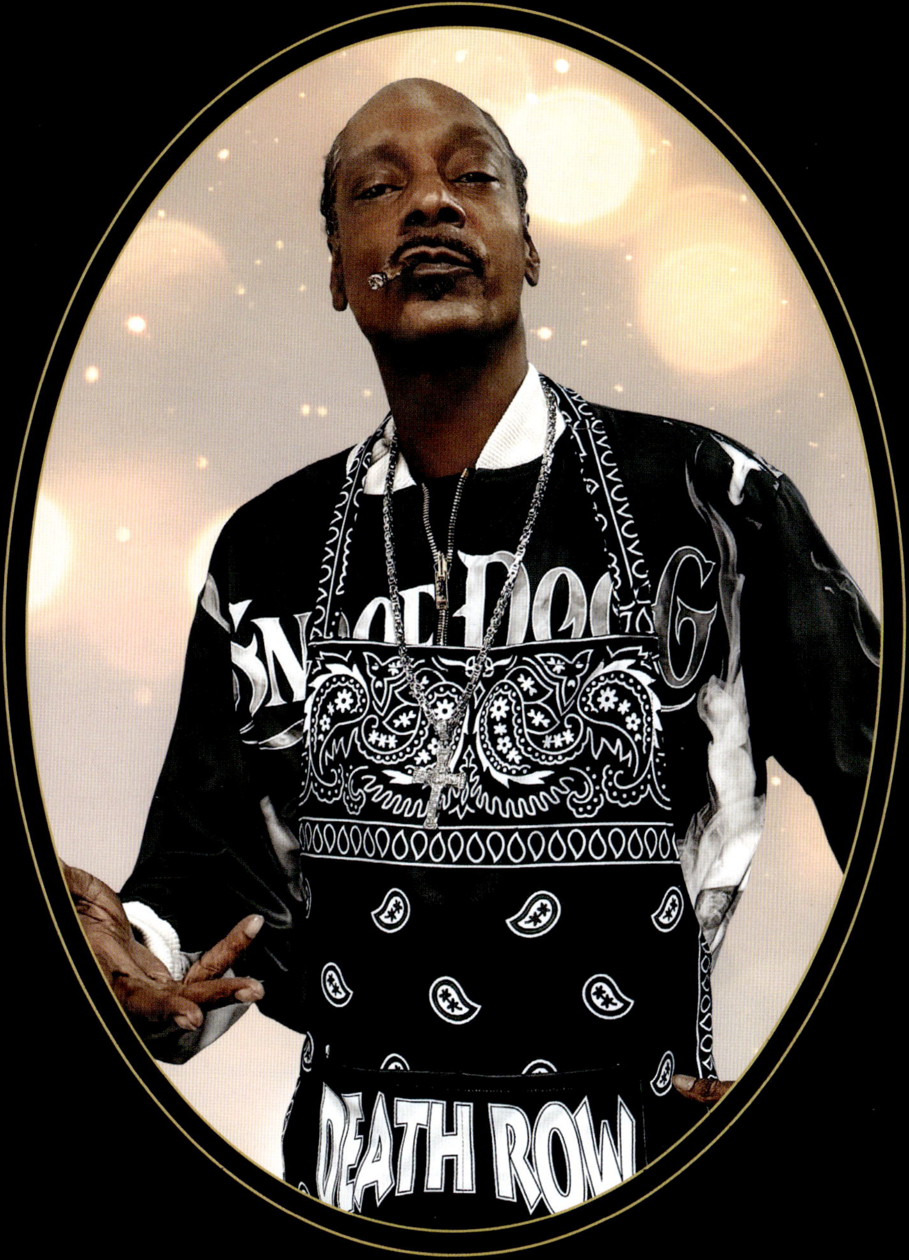
DEATH ROW

Juice (page 169). Roll some Herb 'n' Cheese Fatties to bling out your next party, or fix yourself a bedtime treat with my PB & THC Cups (page 129). Even without weed, these recipes are next level. Just swap in plain ol' butter or oil. It's what you need, ya feel?

Aight. Here's the down low on baking with weed:

STEP 1: Buy your flower. These recipes will work with at least ½ oz [14 g] of your freshest bud. Indica, sativa, it doesn't matter. Head down to Inglewood, where my homies at S.W.E.D. will hook you up.

STEP 2: Ya'll gonna need to **decarb that MJ** before baking it into these fine treats. Your bud has cannabinoids that get you high: you know, that good sh*t. THC (tetrahydrocannabinol) will give you the good giggles and high times. But you have to unlock it first. Cooking up your weed before you bake takes out the CO_2 in THCA and turns it into THC. It activates those compounds so you can ride that buzz.

Think about how those compounds in your bud get lit up when you smoke: same thing here. The weed gets toasted so you can, too. If you want to avoid funking up your house, use an Instant Pot or sous vide machine (page 14). The easiest way of making Cannabutter is to break and bake those nugs in an oven at 220°F [104°C] for about an hour.

STEP 3: Infuse. We keep it real in this book: no grinder, no hash, just infusions. And more time to kick it with the homies. My favorite way to get those cannabinoids into your bake is to use a fat—you know, oil and butter. Cool your decarbed nugs, break them up some more, then simmer with water and butter in a 12-inch covered skillet for about 4 hours. Use cheesecloth or a mesh strainer every 30 minutes or so to keep your butter smooth. Or follow the recipes for butters, tinctures, and oils (pages 15 and 18). My homemade Cannabutter (page 15) is delicious and not too dank when baked into these treats. I like to bring a crock to Martha's for the holidays.

STEP 4: Bake and get baked. Each recipe has three settings: Virgin, Feelin' Good, and Sky High. My treats will dose you up with about 5 mg THC to get you Feelin' Good; if you want more or less, look to the dosage information for guidance. Your ride will vary depending on the bud you bake with. When in doubt, start with a half dose. Infuse the frosting with your Cannabutter (page 15) to kick it up a notch. If you lick the bowl, you're gonna get a Snoop-size dose. Watch out, playas!

STEP 5: Enjoy. Don't forget those good snacks for when the munchies kick in: Dr. Bombay and Rap Snacks are my OGs.

CHAPTER 1

BASICS

Decarbed Cannabis Flower [14]

Cannabis Infusion: Cannabutter,
Cannabis Oil, or Cannabis Glycerine Tincture [15]

Cannabis Grain-Alcohol Tincture [18]

Vanilla Buttercream Frosting [20]

Super-Fudgy Frosting [22]

Pourable Cream Cheese Frosting [24]

Lemon Glaze [26]

DECARBED CANNABIS FLOWER

1. Break up the flower into popcorn-size pieces. Place the pieces in a mason jar just large enough to fit them. For ½ oz [14 g] flower, use a ½ pint [240 ml] jar. If the jar is too big, it will be full of air, and it will float. You don't want that.

2. Place a trivet or steamer basket inside an Instant Pot or pressure cooker, and place the filled jar on top of the trivet. Fill the Instant Pot with water so that the jar is nearly, but not fully, immersed. Pressure-cook the flower on high for 40 minutes. Store the flower in a cool, dark place in the same jar you decarbed it in. It is now ready for infusions.

CANNABIS INFUSION: CANNABUTTER, CANNABIS OIL, OR CANNABIS GLYCERINE TINCTURE

- **MAKES 1 CUP [240 ML]**
- **FOR 24% THC FLOWER, DOSAGE PER TBSP: 105 MG THC**

¼ oz [7 g] Decarbed Cannabis Flower (page 14)

1 cup [220 g] melted unsalted butter, melted coconut oil, vegetable oil, or food-grade glycerin

1. Place the flower in a 1 pt [475 ml] mason jar and pour the butter, oil, or glycerin over the top. Swirl the jar to combine. Place a trivet or steamer basket inside an Instant Pot or pressure cooker, and place the filled jar on top of the trivet. Fill the Instant Pot to the top fill line, and sous vide or slow cook at 185°F [85°C] to make cannabutter and cannabis oils or 150°F [65°C] to make glycerin, for 4 hours. Let the jar cool for 10 minutes.

2. Line a fine-mesh sieve with cheesecloth. Set the sieve over a clean, dark jar and strain the infusion, pressing on the solids with a spatula or wooden spoon to extract all the liquid. Discard the solids. Seal the jar and label it with the date, strain, and potency. Cannabutter will keep in an airtight container in the refrigerator for up to 3 weeks or in the freezer for several months. Cannabis oils and glycerin tincture will last in an airtight container in a cool, dark spot for several months.

CANNABIS INFUSION

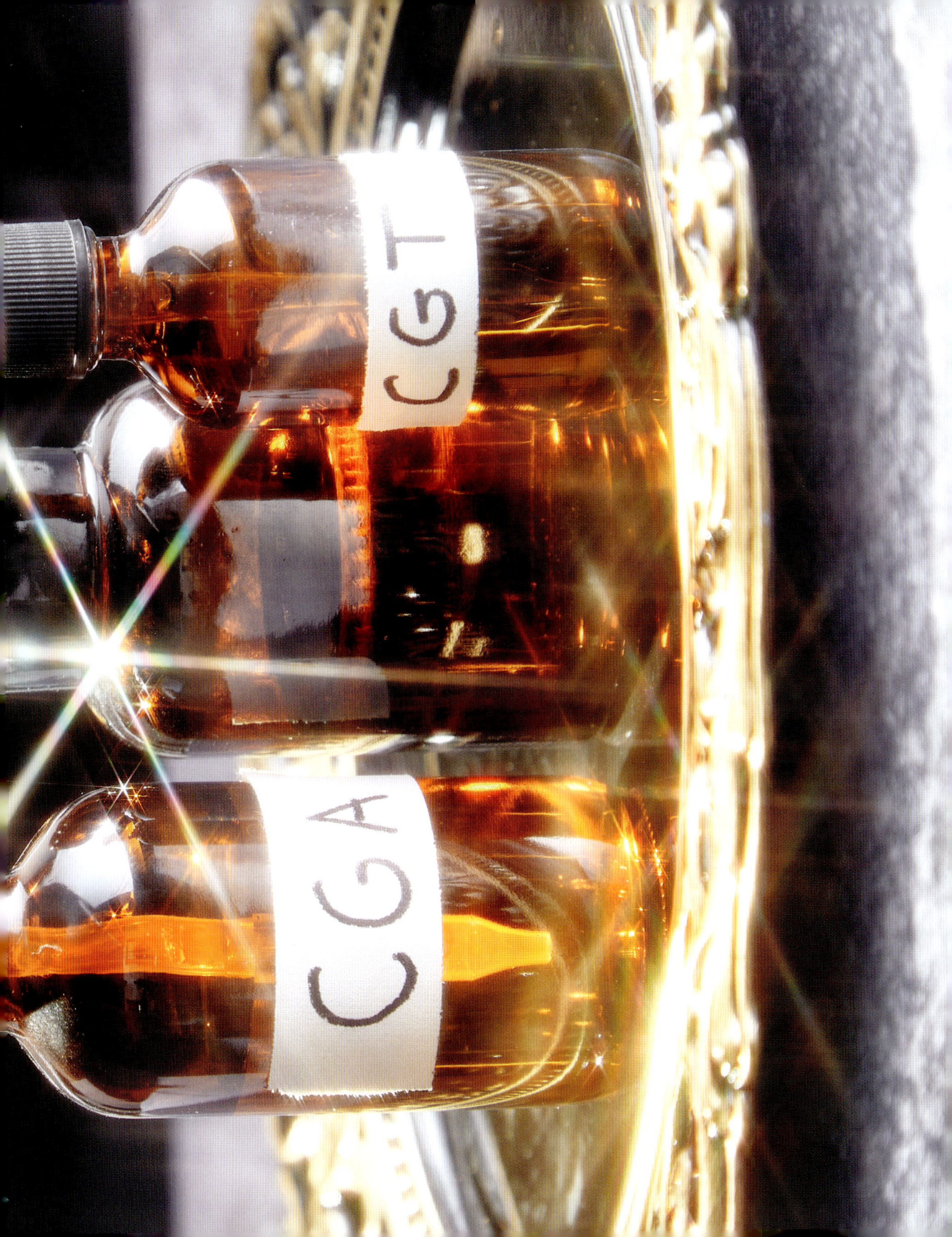
CGT
CGA

CANNABIS GRAIN-ALCOHOL TINCTURE

◆ MAKES ¼ CUP [60 ML]

◆ FOR 24% THC FLOWER, DOSAGE PER ¼ TSP (25 DROPS): 10 MG THC

⅛ oz [3.5 g] Decarbed Cannabis Flower (page 14)

2½ cups [600 ml] Everclear or other 190-proof grain alcohol

1. Grind the flower or break it up into tiny pieces. Add it to an 8 in [20 cm] Pyrex pie plate. Find a saucepan on which the pie plate sits securely, like a lid. Add 3 in [7.5 cm] of water to the saucepan and bring it to a boil. Lower the heat to low, pour the Everclear over the flower, and set the pie plate on top of the saucepan. Watching carefully, let the Everclear evaporate down to ¼ cup [60 ml], checking the amount in a measuring cup if needed, 25 to 30 minutes.

2. Line a fine-mesh sieve with cheesecloth and strain the tincture into a pitcher-style measuring cup, pressing on the solids to extract all the liquid. Discard the solids and, using a small funnel, transfer the tincture to a dark-glass dropper bottle. The tincture will last in the airtight dropper bottle stored in a cool, dark place indefinitely.

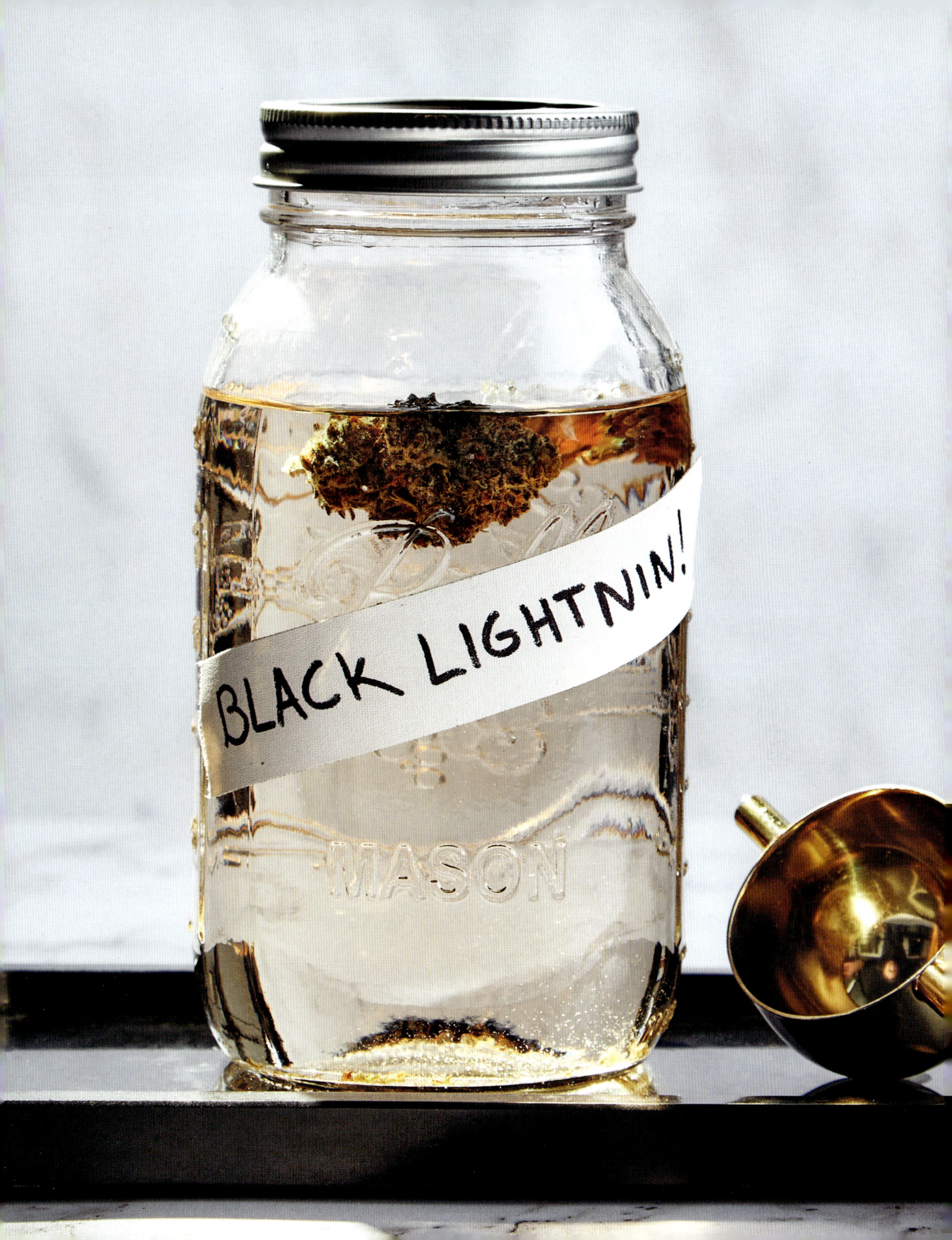
BLACK LIGHTNIN!
MASON

VANILLA BUTTERCREAM FROSTING

✦ **MAKES ABOUT 2 CUPS [480 ML], ENOUGH TO FROST 1 CAKE**
✦ **DOSAGE PER SERVING FOR A 12-SLICE CAKE: 5 TO 6 MG THC***

6 cups [720 g] sifted confectioners' sugar

¾ cup [170 g] unsalted butter, at room temperature

⅜ cup [90 ml] whole milk

1½ tsp vanilla extract

In the bowl of a food processor, combine all the ingredients and pulse until a thick but spreadable frosting forms, about 30 seconds. The frosting will last in an airtight container in the refrigerator for up to 5 days.

---

*Note: To dose the frosting for 1 cake, replace 2 tsp of the unsalted butter with 2 tsp of Cannabutter (page 15). To dose the frosting for the Pumpkin Pot Muffins (page 69), replace 4 tsp unsalted butter with 4 tsp Cannabutter, and use 1 cup [240 ml] of frosting.

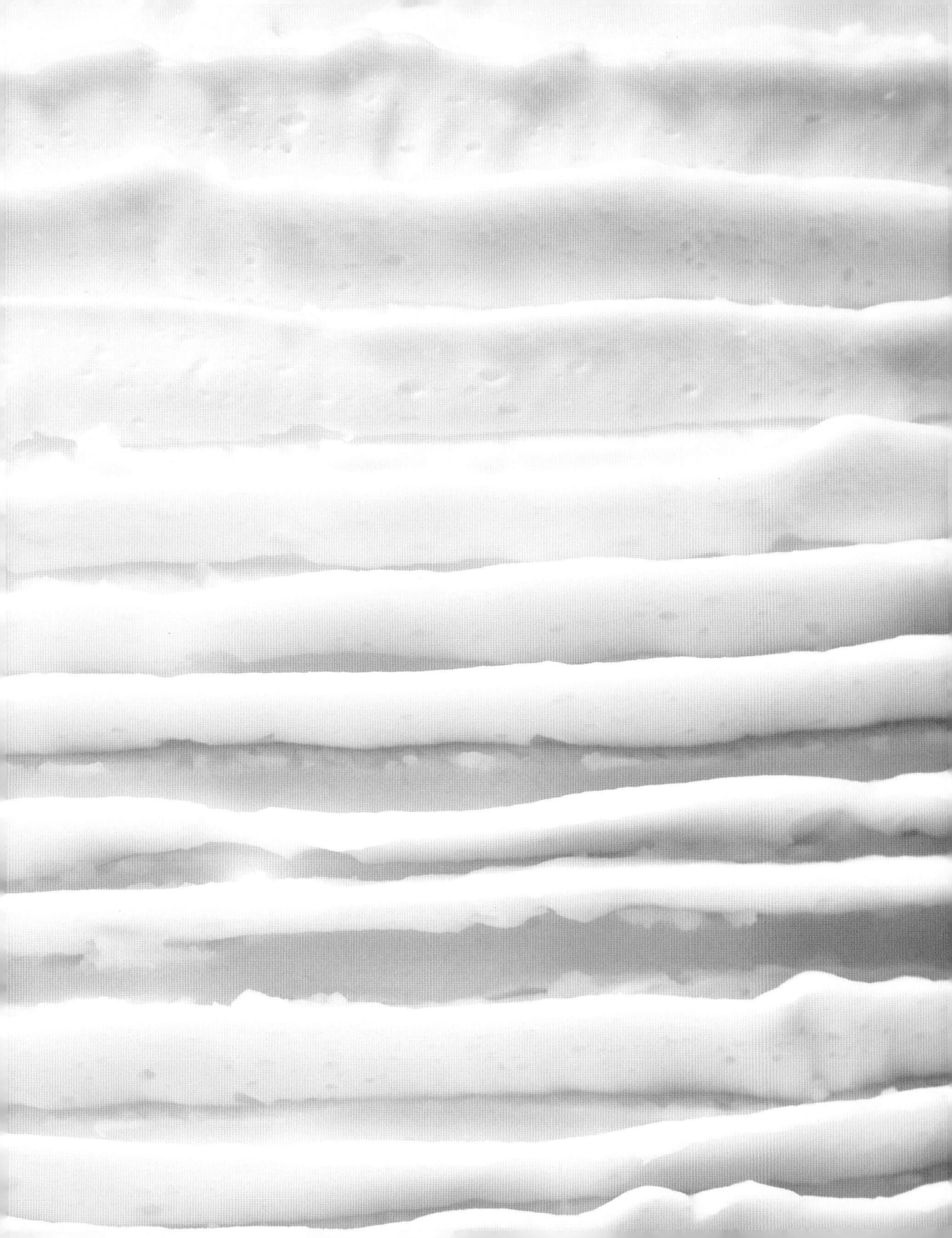

SUPER-FUDGY FROSTING

✦ **MAKES ABOUT 2 CUPS [480 ML], ENOUGH TO FROST 1 CAKE**
✦ **DOSAGE PER SERVING FOR A 12-SLICE CAKE: 5 TO 6 MG THC***

½ cup [110 g] unsalted butter, cubed

6 Tbsp [30 g] unsweetened Dutch-process cocoa powder

⅓ cup [80 ml] whole milk

1 tsp vanilla extract

½ tsp kosher salt

3 cups [360 g] sifted confectioners' sugar

In a medium saucepan over medium-low heat, melt the butter. Stir in the cocoa powder and bring to a simmer. Remove the pan from the heat and whisk in the milk, vanilla, and salt. Whisk in the sugar, 1 cup [120 g] at a time, to form a thick but spreadable frosting. The frosting will last in an airtight container in the refrigerator for up to 5 days.

---

*Note: To dose the frosting for 1 cake, replace 2 tsp of the unsalted butter with 2 tsp of Cannabutter (page 15).

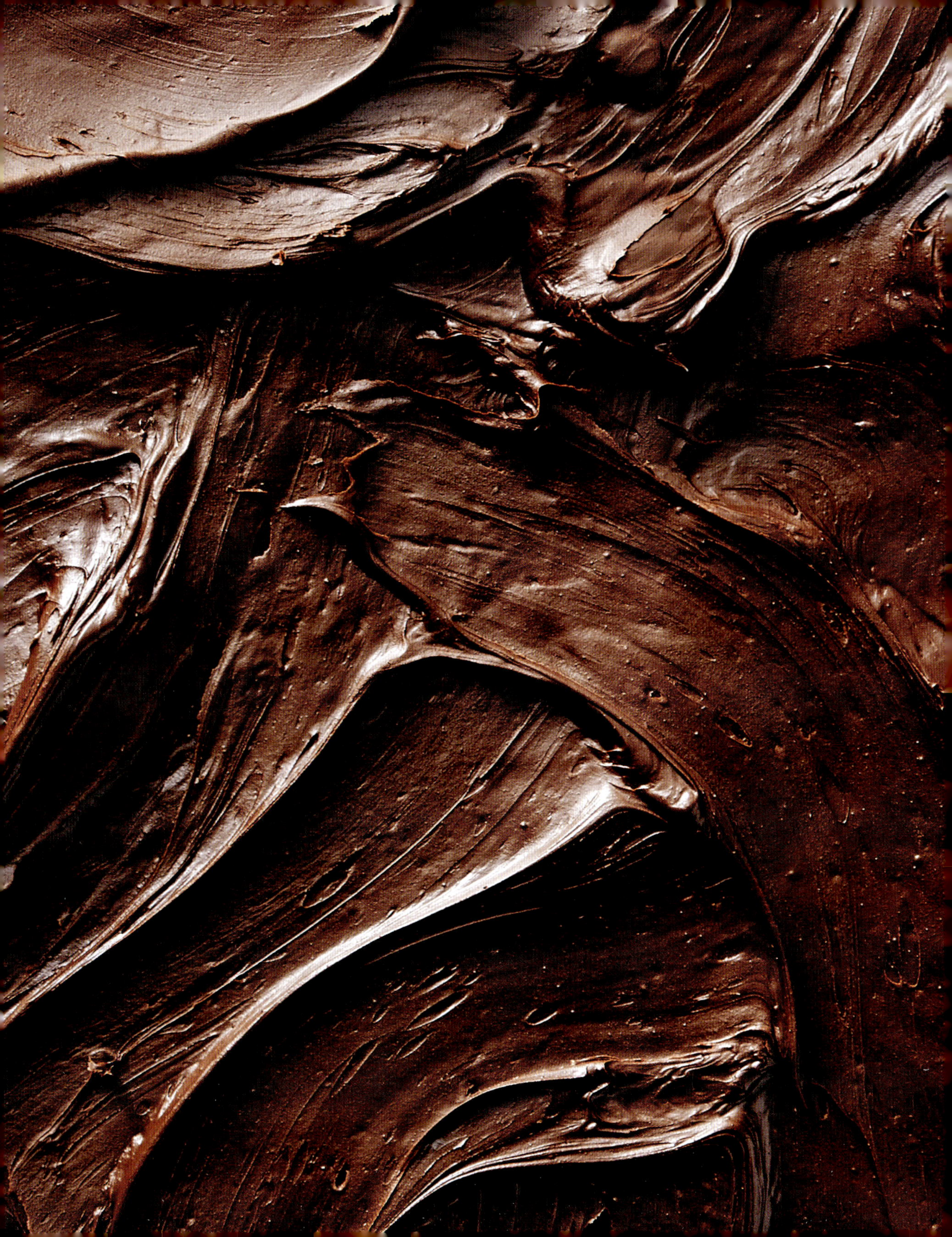

POURABLE CREAM CHEESE FROSTING

◆ **MAKES ABOUT 2 CUPS [480 ML], ENOUGH TO FROST 2 CAKES**
◆ **DOSAGE PER SERVING FOR A 12-SLICE CAKE: 5 TO 6 MG THC***

1 cup [240 g] cream cheese, at room temperature

½ cup [110 g] unsalted butter, at room temperature

½ cup [120 ml] buttermilk

1½ tsp vanilla extract

1 cup [120 g] sifted confectioners' sugar

In the bowl of a stand mixer fitted with the paddle attachment or in a medium bowl with a handheld electric mixer on high speed, beat the cream cheese and butter until fluffy, about 3 minutes. Add the buttermilk and vanilla and beat until fully combined. Add the confectioners' sugar and beat to form a smooth and pourable frosting, about 3 minutes. The frosting will last in an airtight container in the refrigerator for up to 5 days.

---

*Note: To dose the frosting to pour over the Red Velvet Blundt Cakes (page 85), replace 5 tsp of the unsalted butter with 5 tsp of Cannabutter (page 15) and use half the frosting.

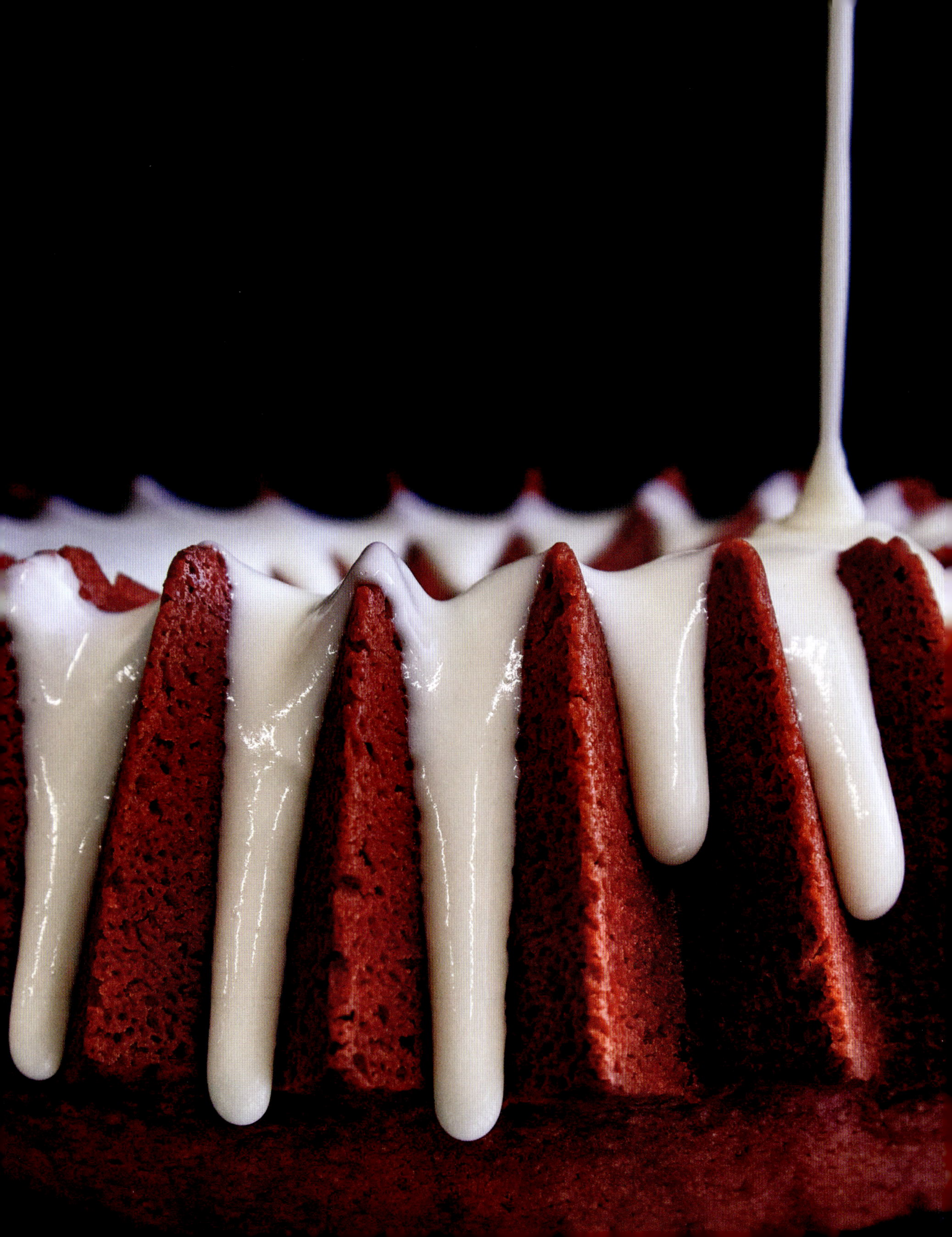

Lemon Glaze

- MAKES ABOUT 1 CUP [240 ML], ENOUGH TO FROST 12 MUFFINS OR GLAZE 36 SUGAR COOKIES
- DOSAGE PER SERVING FOR A 12-SLICE CAKE: 5 TO 6 MG THC*

1 cup [120 g] sifted confectioners' sugar

2 Tbsp fresh lemon juice

In a small bowl, whisk the confectioners' sugar with the lemon juice until a thick glaze forms. The glaze will last in an airtight container in the refrigerator for up to 1 week.

---

*Note: If dosing this to glaze the Sugar Cookies Two Ways (page 36), add 1 Tbsp Cannabis Glycerine Tincture and increase the confectioners' sugar by ½ cup [60 g]. If dosing this to glaze the Lemon Poppy Seed Pot Muffins (page 72), add 2 tsp Cannabis Glycerine Tincture.

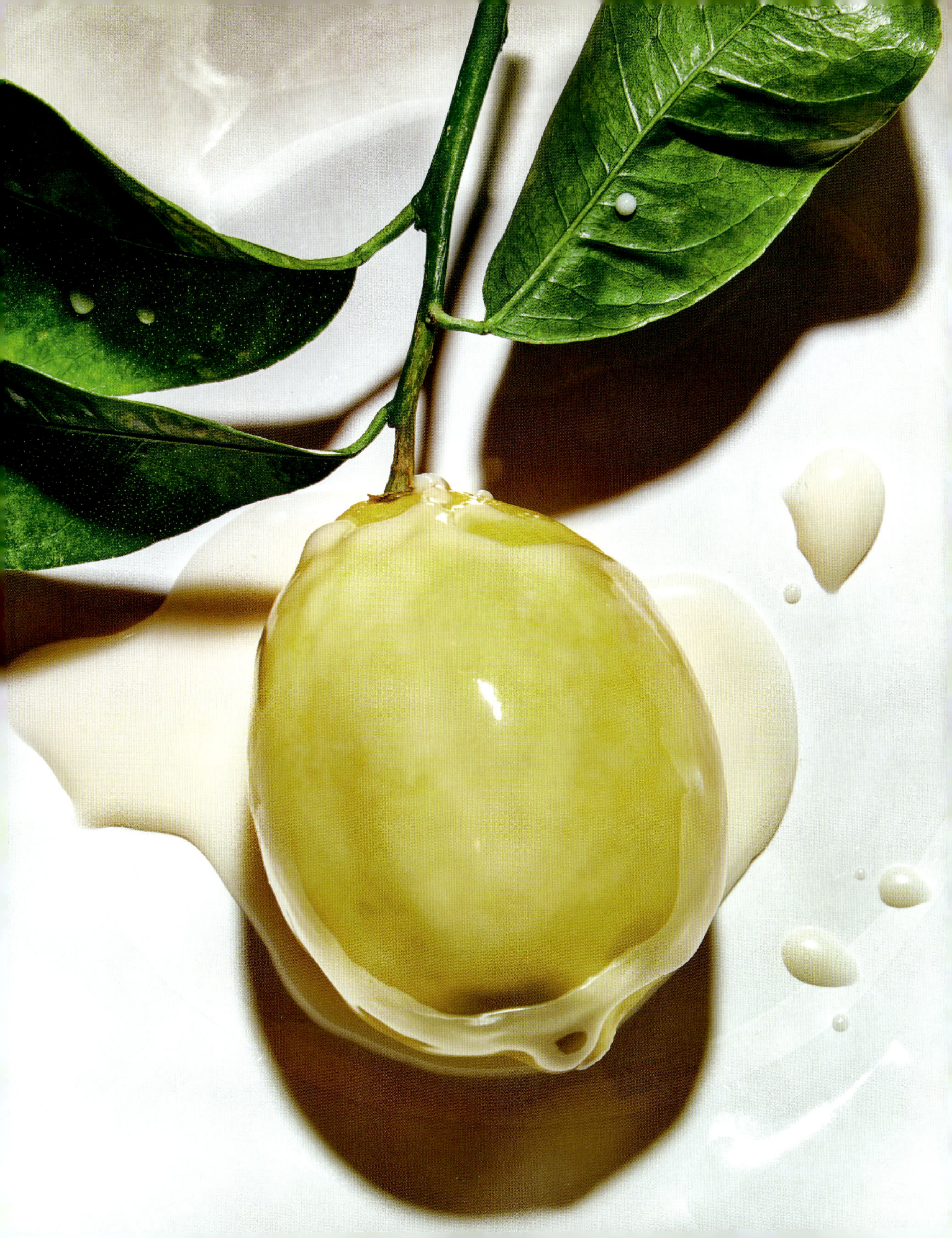

CHAPTER 2

COOKIES

Chocolate Chip Cookies [30]

Oatmeal Raisin Cookies [33]

Sugar Cookies Two Ways [36]

Snooperdoodles [40]

Ganja Snaps [43]

Nutter Butter Stoner Cookies [46]

Connoisseur Cookies [50]

CHOCOLATE CHIP COOKIES

- **MAKES ABOUT 3 DOZEN COOKIES**
- **SERVING SIZE: 1 COOKIE**
- **DOSAGE PER SERVING: FEELIN' GOOD (5 TO 6 MG THC); FOR SKY HIGH (10 TO 12 MG) USE 9 TBSP UNSALTED BUTTER AND 2 TBSP CANNABUTTER**
- **FOR VIRGIN (0 MG) USE 11 TBSP UNSALTED BUTTER ONLY**

1 cup [120 g] chopped walnuts (optional)

2 cups [280 g] all-purpose flour

1 tsp baking soda

1 tsp kosher salt

1½ cups [300 g] packed dark brown sugar

½ cup [100 g] granulated sugar

10 Tbsp [145 g] unsalted butter, cubed, at room temperature

1 Tbsp Cannabutter (page 15), at room temperature

2 large eggs

2 tsp vanilla extract

1½ cups [270 g] semisweet chocolate chips

Flaky sea salt, for topping

CONTINUED →

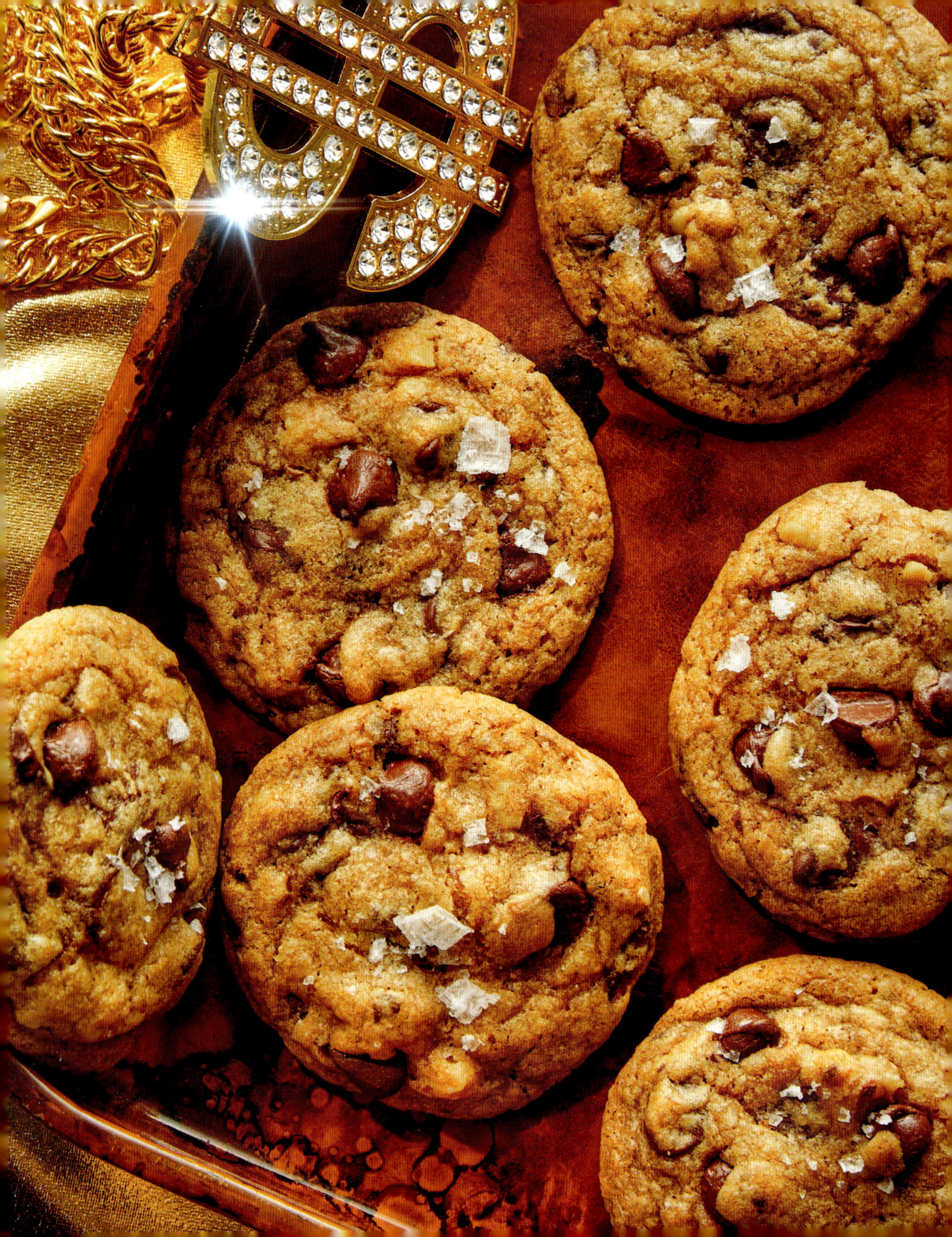

1. Preheat the oven to 350°F [180°C]. Line a baking sheet with parchment paper or a silicone baking mat.

2. Spread the walnuts, if using, on the prepared baking sheet and toast until fragrant and starting to glisten, 10 minutes. Cool to room temperature and transfer to a small bowl.

3. In a separate small bowl, whisk together the flour, baking soda, and kosher salt.

4. In the bowl of a stand mixer fitted with the paddle attachment or a medium bowl with a handheld electric mixer on medium speed, cream the sugars, unsalted butter, and cannabutter together until fluffy. Beat in the eggs and vanilla.

5. Add the flour mixture and beat on low speed until well combined. Stir in the chocolate chips and walnuts with a spatula or wooden spoon.

6. Working in batches, scoop 1 heaping Tbsp of the dough at a time and place about 2 in [5 cm] apart onto the prepared baking sheet. Sprinkle each with flaky sea salt.

7. Bake for 5 minutes on the middle rack, remove the pan from the oven, and drop it (like it's hot) from a few inches above the countertop to give the cookies ripples and crispy edges. Return the pan to the oven, rotating it 180 degrees, and bake for 5 minutes more.

8. Cool the cookies on the baking sheet for 1 minute, then transfer them to a wire rack to cool fully. The cookies will last in an airtight container at room temperature for up to 5 days or frozen for up to 1 month.

9. Repeat with the remaining dough or shape it into 1 Tbsp balls and store them in a Ziploc bag. The dough balls will last in the freezer for up to 1 month.

OATMEAL RAISIN COOKIES

- **MAKES ABOUT 4 DOZEN COOKIES**
- **SERVING SIZE: 1 COOKIE**
- **DOSAGE PER SERVING: FEELIN' GOOD (5 TO 6 MG THC); FOR SKY HIGH (10 TO 12 MG) USE 10 TBSP UNSALTED BUTTER AND 3 TBSP CANNABUTTER**
- **FOR VIRGIN (0 MG) USE 14 TBSP UNSALTED BUTTER ONLY**

1 cup [120 g] chopped pecans (optional)

½ cup [70 g] golden raisins

½ cup [70 g] dark raisins

3 cups [720 ml] boiling water

1½ cups [210 g] all-purpose flour

1 tsp baking soda

1 tsp ground cinnamon

1 tsp kosher salt

¼ tsp allspice

12 Tbsp [170 g] unsalted butter, at room temperature

7 tsp Cannabutter (page 15), at room temperature

⅔ cup [130 g] packed brown sugar

½ cup [100 g] granulated sugar

2 eggs

1 Tbsp molasses

1 tsp vanilla extract

3 cups [300 g] rolled oats

CONTINUED →

1. Preheat the oven to 350°F [180°C]. Line a baking sheet with parchment paper or a silicone baking mat. Spread the pecans, if using, on the prepared baking sheet and toast until fragrant, about 7 minutes. Cool to room temperature and transfer to a small bowl.

2. Place the golden and dark raisins in another small bowl and pour the boiling water over the top to cover. Let them plump while you make the dough.

3. In another small bowl, whisk together the flour, baking soda, cinnamon, salt, and allspice.

4. In the bowl of a stand mixer fitted with the paddle attachment or in a medium bowl with a handheld electric mixer on medium speed, cream the unsalted butter, cannabutter, and both sugars until fluffy. Beat in the eggs, molasses, and vanilla.

5. Add the flour mixture and beat until fully combined.

6. Drain the raisins, pressing them with a wooden spoon to release most of the water. Add the oats, raisins, and pecans, if using, to the dough and mix until fully combined.

7. Working in batches, scoop 1 heaping Tbsp of the dough at a time about 2 in [5 cm] apart onto the prepared baking sheet. Bake for 5 minutes, rotate the baking sheet 180 degrees, and bake for 5 minutes more, until fragrant and cooked through but still soft.

8. Cool the cookies on the baking sheet for 1 minute, then transfer to a wire rack to cool fully. The cookies will last in an airtight container at room temperature for up to 5 days or frozen for up to 1 month.

9. Repeat with the remaining dough or shape it into 1 Tbsp balls and store them in a Ziploc bag. The dough balls will last in the freezer for up to 1 month.

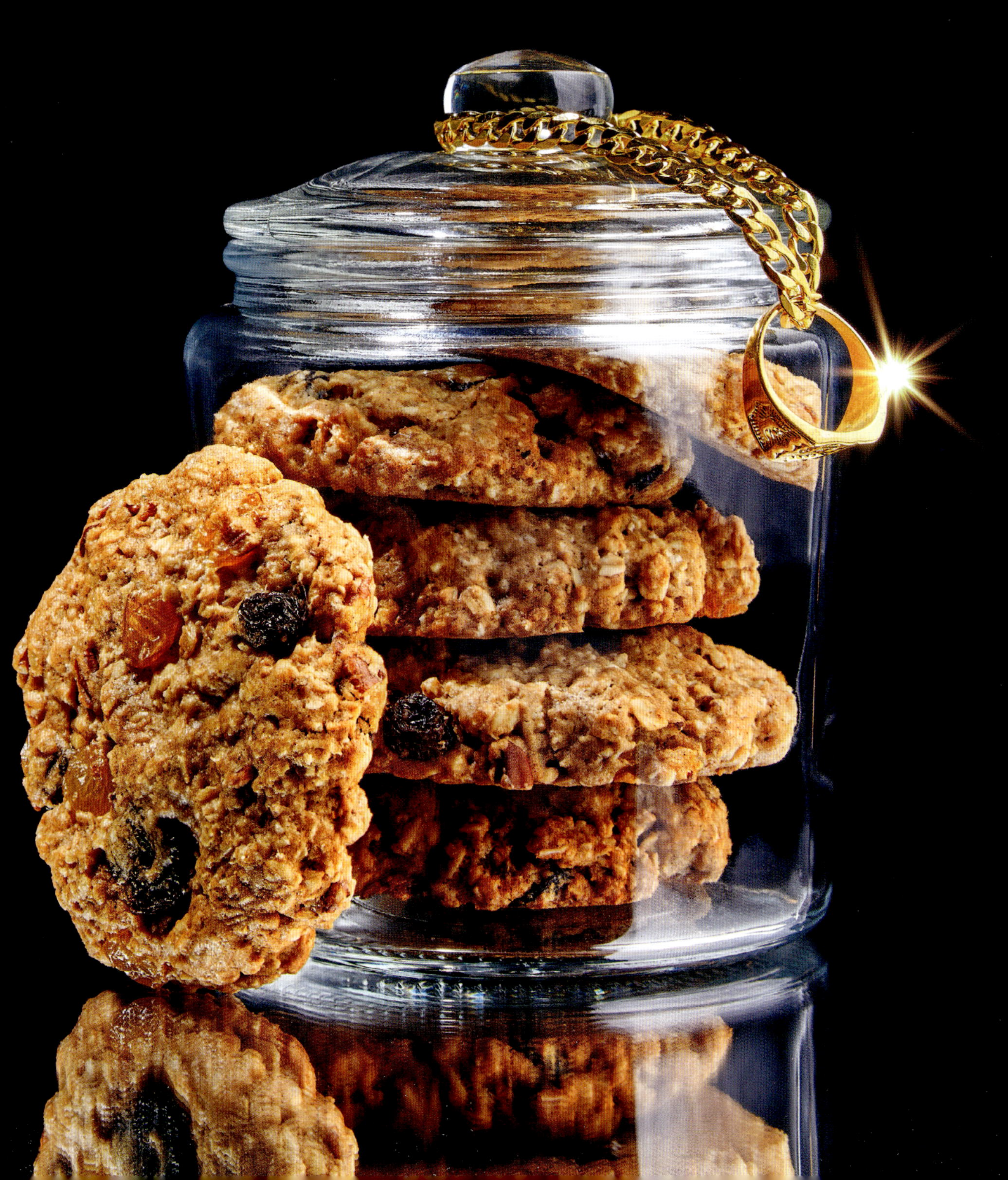

Sugar Cookies Two Ways

- **MAKES ABOUT 6 DOZEN COOKIES**
- **SERVING SIZE: 2 COOKIES**
- **DOSAGE PER SERVING: FEELIN' GOOD (5 TO 6 MG THC); FOR SKY HIGH (10 TO 12 MG) USE 12 TBSP UNSALTED BUTTER AND 4 TBSP CANNABUTTER***
- **FOR VIRGIN (0 MG) USE 16 TBSP UNSALTED BUTTER ONLY**

3 cups [420 g] all-purpose flour

1 tsp baking powder

¾ tsp kosher salt

¼ tsp baking soda

1¼ cups [250 g] granulated sugar

14 Tbsp [190 g] unsalted butter, at room temperature

2 Tbsp Cannabutter (page 15), at room temperature

¼ cup [60 g] cream cheese, at room temperature

1 tsp vanilla extract

¼ tsp almond extract

1 large egg

¾ cup [150 g] colored sugar, for dredging

Lemon Glaze (page 26), for drizzling (optional, see Note)

Lemon zest, for garnish

1. Preheat the oven to 350°F [180°C]. Line a baking sheet with parchment paper or a silicone baking mat.

2. In a medium bowl, whisk together the flour, baking powder, salt, and baking soda.

3. In the bowl of a stand mixer fitted with the paddle attachment or in a medium bowl with a handheld electric mixer on low speed, cream the granulated sugar, unsalted butter, and cannabutter together until fluffy.

4. Add the cream cheese, vanilla, almond extract, and egg and beat until well combined. Add the flour mixture and mix just until a smooth dough forms.

5. Place the colored sugar in a bowl. Scooping 1 Tbsp at a time, form the dough into balls. Roll half the balls in the colored sugar.

6. Working in batches, scoop 1 heaping Tbsp of the remaining dough at a time about 2 in [5 cm] apart onto the prepared baking sheet. Using the bottom of a measuring cup or a rocks glass, press the balls to flatten them into ¼ in [6 mm] thick discs.

7. Bake until golden at the edges and slightly firm to the touch in the center, 10 to 12 minutes. Cool on the baking sheet for 1 minute, then transfer to a wire rack to cool fully.

8. Drizzle the lemon glaze over the undredged cookies and garnish them with lemon zest. Let the glaze set, 10 minutes. The cookies will last in an airtight container at room temperature for up to 3 days or in the freezer for up to 1 month.

9. Repeat with the remaining dough or shape the remaining dough into 1 Tbsp balls and store them in a Ziploc bag. The dough will last in the freezer for up to 1 month.

---

*Note: Swap out cannabutter for unsalted butter and ice these cookies with dosed Lemon Glaze for the same dosage per serving. Using cannabutter and the Lemon Glaze will double your dose.

SUGAR COOKIES

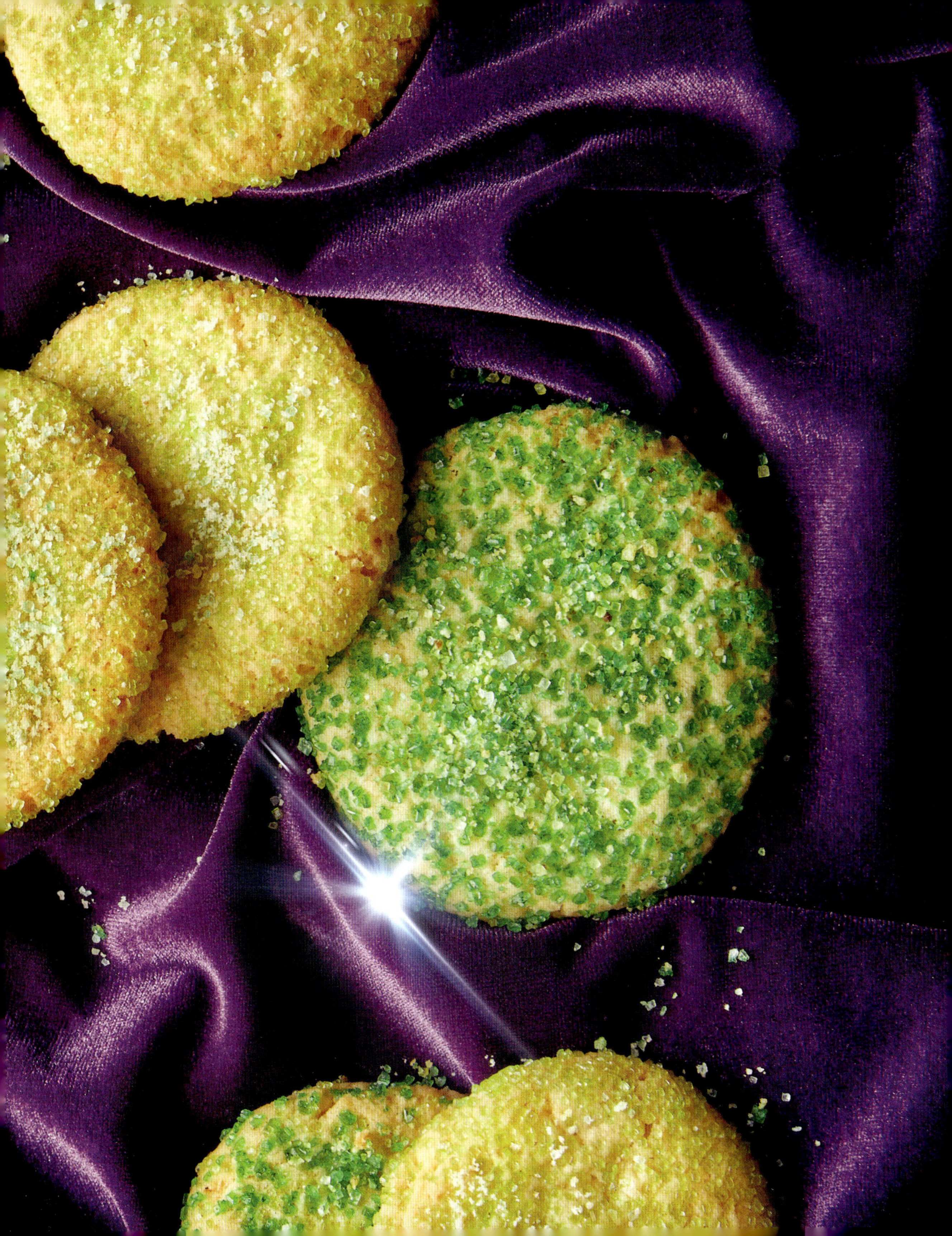

SNOOPER-DOODLES

- **MAKES ABOUT 4 DOZEN COOKIES**
- **SERVING SIZE: 1 COOKIE**
- **DOSAGE PER SERVING: FEELIN' GOOD (5 TO 6 MG THC); FOR SKY HIGH (10 TO 12 MG) USE 10 TBSP UNSALTED BUTTER AND 4½ TBSP CANNABUTTER**
- **FOR VIRGIN (0 MG) USE 14 TBSP UNSALTED BUTTER ONLY**

3 cups [420 g] all-purpose flour

2 tsp cream of tartar

1 tsp baking soda

½ tsp kosher salt

1¾ cups [350 g] sugar

12 Tbsp [170 g] unsalted butter, at room temperature

2½ Tbsp Cannabutter (page 15), at room temperature

2 eggs

5 tsp ground cinnamon

1½ tsp vanilla extract

CONTINUED ➜

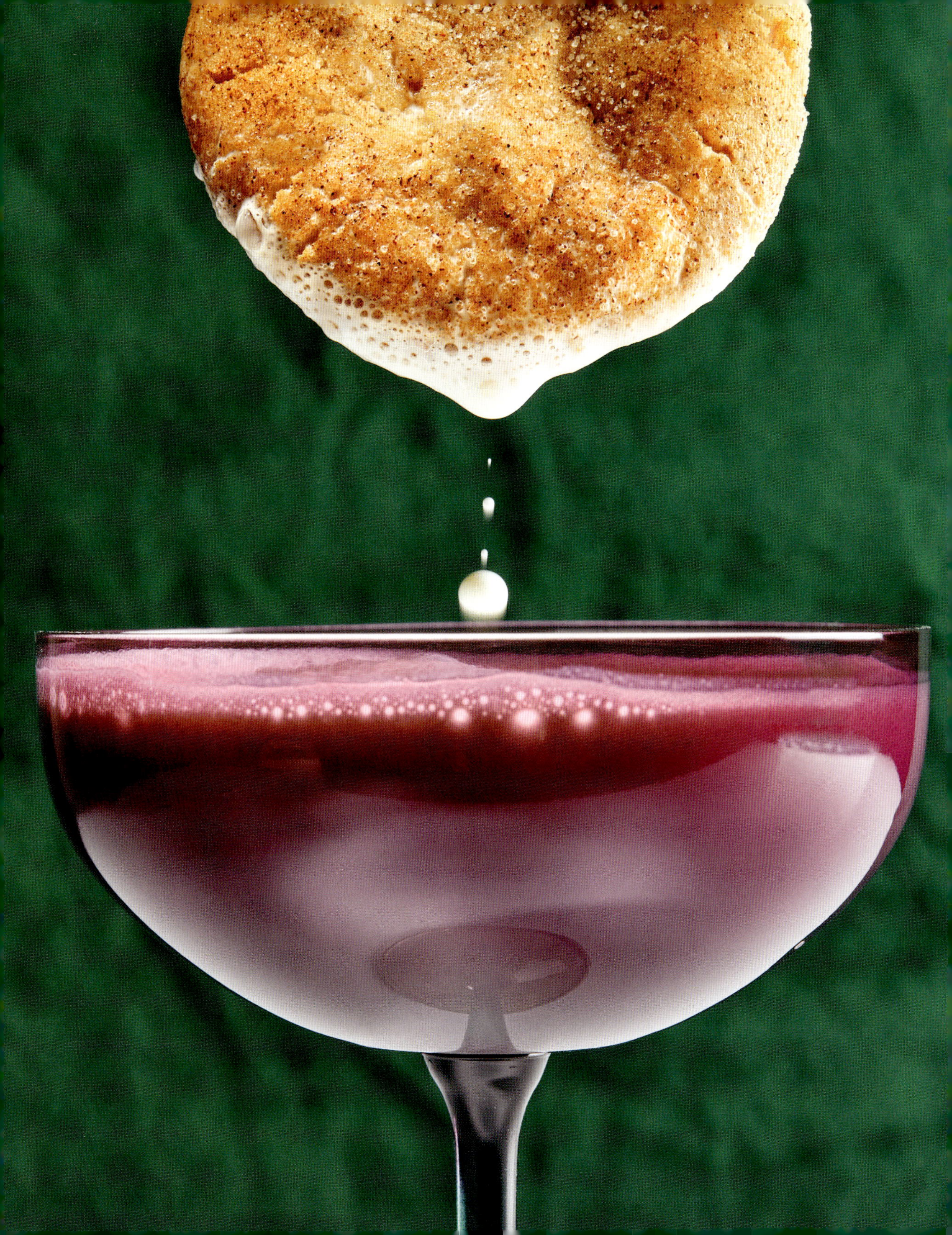

1. In a small bowl, whisk together the flour, cream of tartar, baking soda, and salt.

2. In the bowl of a stand mixer fitted with the paddle attachment or in a medium bowl with a handheld electric mixer on medium speed, cream 1½ cups [300 g] of the sugar, the unsalted butter, and the cannabutter together until fluffy.

3. Beat in the eggs, 2 tsp of the cinnamon, and the vanilla. Add the flour mixture and beat until a dough just comes together, about 2 minutes. Chill the dough for 30 minutes.

4. Preheat the oven to 350°F [180°C]. Line a baking sheet with parchment paper or a silicone baking mat.

5. In a small bowl, whisk together the remaining ¼ cup [50 g] of sugar and 3 tsp of cinnamon.

6. Working in batches, scoop 1 Tbsp of dough at a time and form into balls. Roll the balls in the cinnamon sugar.

7. Place the dough balls 2 in [5 cm] apart on the prepared baking sheet, pressing slightly to flatten the tops.

8. Bake for 10 minutes, until golden at the edges. Cool on the baking sheet for 1 minute, then transfer the cookies to a wire rack to cool fully. The cookies will last in an airtight container at room temperature for up to 3 days or in the freezer for up to 1 month.

9. Repeat with the remaining dough or shape it into slightly flattened balls and store them in a Ziploc bag. The dough will last in the freezer for up to 1 month.

GANJA SNAPS

- **MAKES ABOUT 6 DOZEN COOKIES**
- **SERVING SIZE: 2 COOKIES**
- **DOSAGE PER SERVING: FEELIN' GOOD (5 TO 6 MG THC); FOR SKY HIGH (10 TO 12 MG) USE 9 TBSP UNSALTED BUTTER AND 4 TBSP CANNABUTTER**
- **FOR VIRGIN (0 MG) USE 13 TBSP UNSALTED BUTTER ONLY**

2 cups [280 g] all-purpose flour, plus more for dusting

1 Tbsp ground ginger

1½ tsp ground cinnamon

½ tsp baking powder

¼ tsp white pepper

⅛ tsp cloves

1 cup [200 g] packed dark brown sugar

11 Tbsp [155 g] unsalted butter, at room temperature

2 Tbsp Cannabutter (page 15), at room temperature

1 large egg

¾ tsp peeled, grated fresh ginger

¾ tsp lemon zest

Turbinado sugar, for garnish (optional)

CONTINUED ➜

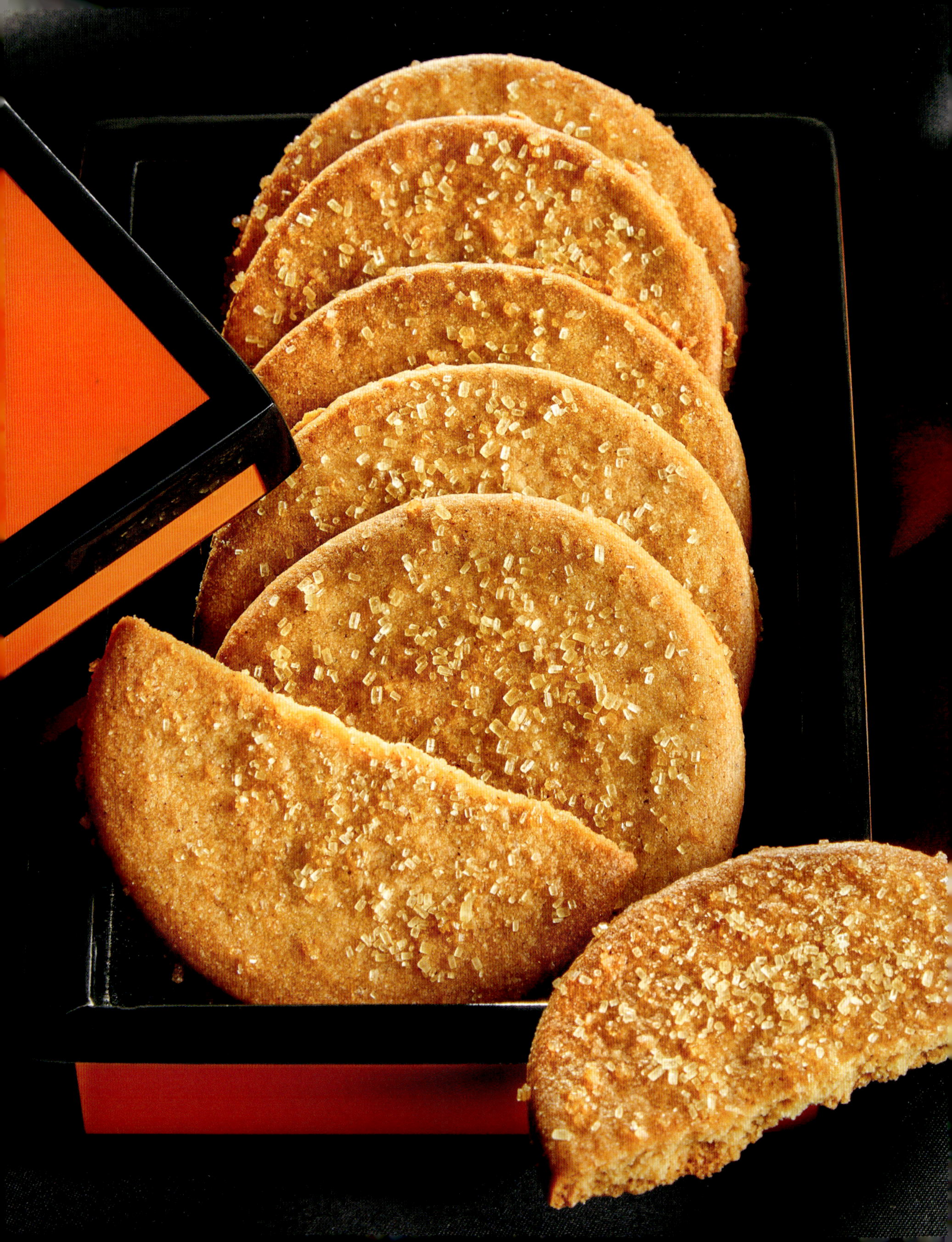

1. In a medium bowl, whisk together the flour, ground ginger, cinnamon, baking powder, white pepper, and cloves.

2. In the bowl of a stand mixer fitted with the paddle attachment or in a medium bowl with an electric handheld mixer on medium speed, cream the brown sugar, unsalted butter, and cannabutter together until fluffy. Beat in the egg, fresh ginger, and lemon zest.

3. Add the flour mixture and beat until the dough just comes together, about 2 minutes.

4. Form the dough into 3 discs, wrap in parchment paper or plastic wrap, and chill in the refrigerator for 1 hour.

5. Preheat the oven to 350°F [180°C]. Line a baking sheet with parchment paper or a silicone baking mat.

6. On a lightly floured surface with a lightly floured rolling pin, roll 1 disc out to ⅛ in [4 mm]. Working in batches, use a 3 in [7.5 cm] marijuana-leaf or 2 in [5 cm] round cookie cutter to cut out the cookies, rerolling scraps to use up the remaining dough.

7. Transfer the cookies to the prepared baking sheet. They don't spread, so you can place them closer together.

8. Sprinkle the cookies with turbinado sugar, if using. Bake for 6 minutes, rotate the pan 180 degrees, then bake for another 6 minutes until crisp and dark brown.

9. Cool on the baking sheet for 1 minute, then transfer the cookies to a wire rack to cool fully. The cookies will last in an airtight container at room temperature for up to 3 days or in the freezer for up to 1 month.

10. Repeat with the remaining dough or save it for later. A disc of dough will last, wrapped tightly with plastic wrap, in the refrigerator for up to 2 days or in the freezer for up to 1 month. Defrost it in the refrigerator overnight, then leave it on the countertop for 30 minutes to soften before rolling.

NUTTER BUTTER STONER COOKIES

- ◆ MAKES 20 COOKIES
- ◆ SERVING SIZE: 1 COOKIE
- ◆ DOSAGE PER SERVING: FEELIN' GOOD (5 TO 6 MG THC); FOR SKY HIGH (10 TO 12 MG) USE 6 TBSP UNSALTED BUTTER AND 2 TBSP CANNABUTTER
- ◆ FOR VIRGIN (0 MG) USE 8 TBSP UNSALTED BUTTER ONLY

FOR THE COOKIES

1½ cups [210 g] all-purpose flour

1 tsp baking soda

1 tsp cornstarch

½ tsp kosher salt

½ cup [100 g] packed light brown sugar

½ cup [100 g] packed dark brown sugar

7 Tbsp [100 g] unsalted butter, at room temperature

1 Tbsp Cannabutter (page 15), at room temperature

1 cup [260 g] creamy peanut butter

1 egg

1 tsp vanilla extract

FOR THE CREAM

1 cup [120 g] sifted confectioners' sugar

¾ cup [195 g] creamy peanut butter

6 Tbsp [90 ml] half-and-half

¾ tsp vanilla extract

TO MAKE THE COOKIES

1. Preheat the oven to 350°F [180°C]. Line a baking sheet with parchment paper or a silicone baking mat.

2. In a medium bowl, whisk together the flour, baking soda, cornstarch, and salt.

3. In the bowl of a stand mixer fitted with the paddle attachment or in a medium bowl with a handheld electric mixer on medium-low speed, cream the light brown sugar, dark brown sugar, unsalted butter, and cannabutter until fluffy. Beat in the peanut butter, egg, and vanilla.

4. Add the flour mixture and beat until a dough comes together, about 2 minutes.

5. Working in batches and scooping 1 Tbsp at a time, roll the dough on the prepared baking sheet into 3 in [7.5 cm] logs, leaving 2 in [5 cm] of space between each log.

6. Flatten the logs into long ovals and pinch the middle of each to make a peanut shape. Using the back of a fork, create hash marks on each half of the peanut shape.

7. Bake, rotating the pan 180 degrees midway through, until crisp and golden brown at the edges but still tender in the middle, 10 to 12 minutes.

8. Cool on the baking sheet for 1 minute, then transfer the cookies to a wire rack to cool fully. The cookies will last in an airtight container on the countertop for up to 3 days or in the freezer for up to 1 month.

TO MAKE THE CREAM AND FILL THE COOKIES

1. In the bowl of a stand mixer fitted with the paddle attachment or pulsing in a food processor, cream all the ingredients together to form a sticky cream.

2. Transfer the cream to a piping bag fitted with a star tip or a Ziploc bag and cut the tip of the piping bag or a corner of the Ziploc bag. Turn half the cookies over and pipe 2 tsp of cream onto each upside-down cookie. Top with the remaining cookies.

3. The cookies will last in an airtight container at room temperature for up to 3 days or in the freezer for up to 1 month.

NUTTER BUTTER STONER COOKIES

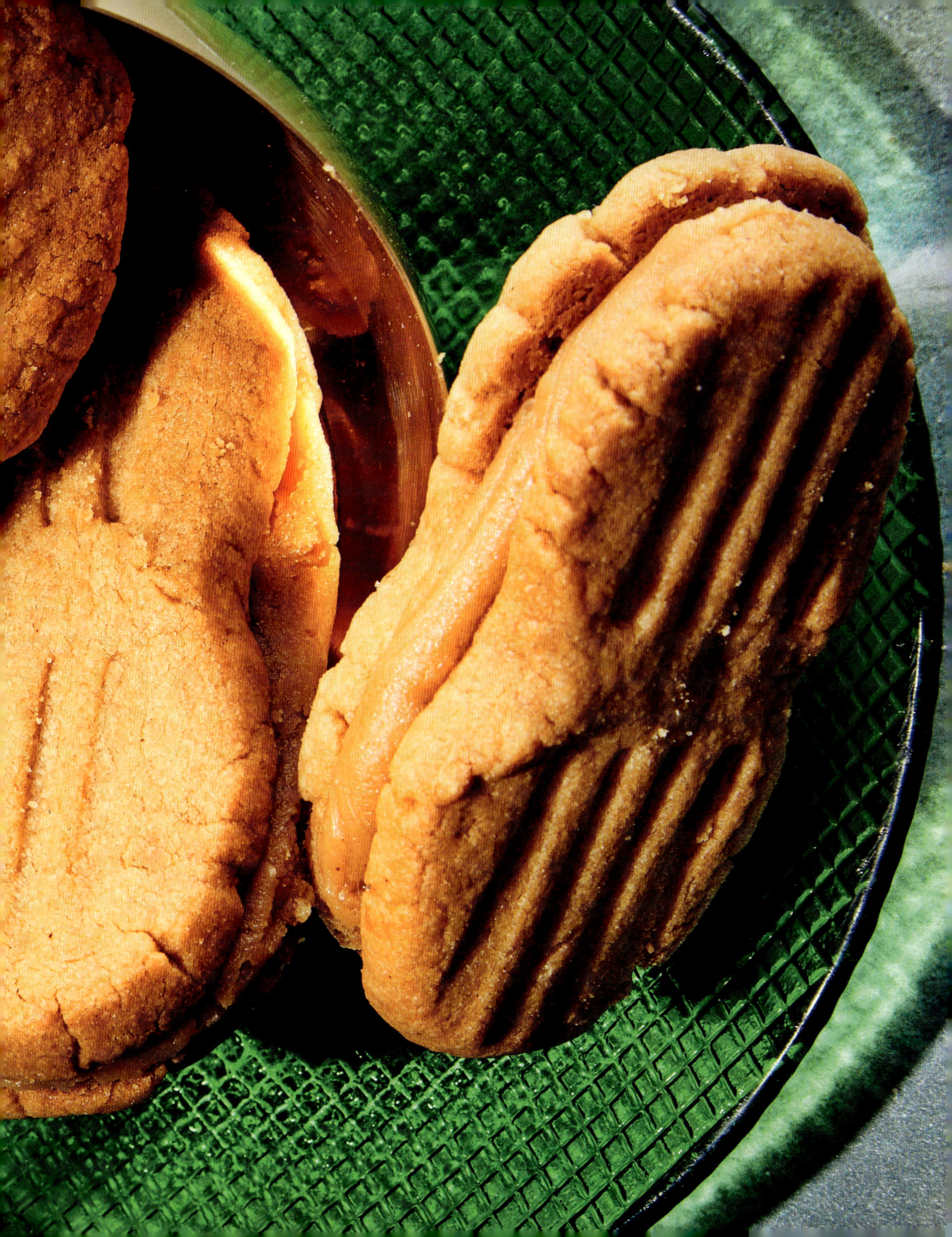

Connoisseur Cookies

- **MAKES ABOUT 3 DOZEN COOKIES**
- **SERVING SIZE: 1 COOKIE**
- **DOSAGE PER SERVING: FEELIN' GOOD (5 TO 6 MG THC); FOR SKY HIGH (10 TO 12 MG) USE 12 TBSP UNSALTED BUTTER AND 2 TBSP CANNABUTTER**
- **FOR VIRGIN (0 MG) USE 14 TBSP UNSALTED BUTTER ONLY**

2¼ cups [315 g] flour

1 tsp kosher salt

1 tsp baking soda

14 Tbsp [190 g] unsalted butter, at room temperature

4 tsp Cannabutter (page 15), at room temperature

⅔ cup [130 g] granulated sugar

⅔ cup [130 g] packed dark brown sugar

2 large eggs

1 tsp vanilla extract

4 oz [115 g] Plain or Peanut M&Ms

2 oz [55 g] pretzel sticks or mini pretzels, broken into ½ in [13 mm] pieces

2 oz [55 g] ripple potato chips, lightly crushed

Edible gold leaf, to garnish (optional)

1. Preheat the oven to 350°F [180°C]. Line a baking sheet with parchment paper or a silicone baking mat.

2. In a medium bowl, whisk together the flour, salt, and baking soda.

3. In the bowl of a stand mixer fitted with the paddle attachment or in a medium bowl with a handheld electric electric mixer on medium speed, cream the unsalted butter, cannabutter, and both sugars until fluffy. Beat in the eggs and vanilla.

4. Add the flour mixture and beat until a dough comes together, about 2 minutes. With a spatula or wooden spoon, fold in the M&Ms, pretzels, and potato chips.

5. Working in batches, scoop 1 Tbsp of the dough at a time about 2 in [5 cm] apart onto the prepared baking sheet. Feel free to add that gold leaf, you dig. Bake for 8 minutes, rotate the baking sheet 180 degrees, and bake for 5 to 7 minutes more, until golden brown.

6. Cool on the baking sheet for 1 minute, then transfer the cookies to a wire rack to cool fully. The cookies will last in an airtight container at room temperature for up to 5 days or in the freezer for up to 1 month.

7. Repeat with the remaining dough or shape it into 1 Tbsp balls and store them in a Ziploc bag. The dough balls will last in the freezer for up to 1 month.

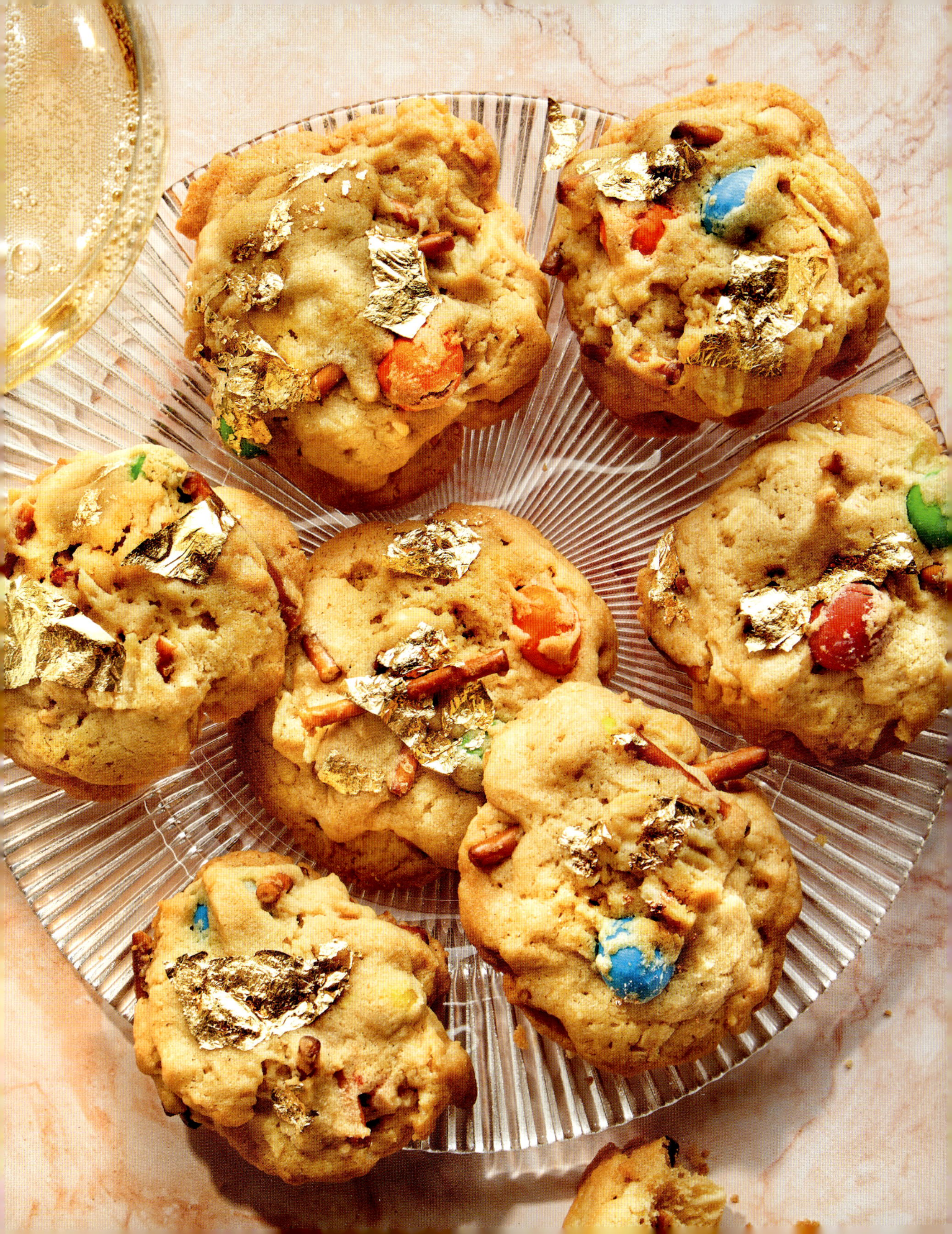

CHAPTER 3

BROWNIES, BLONDIES, AND MUFFINS

Dank Double-Chocolate Brownies 55

Peppermint Pot Brownies 57

Loaded Brown-Butter Blondies 60

Fruit Loops Bars with Benefits 64

PB, C, and J Bars 67

Pumpkin Pot Muffins 69

Lemon Poppy Seed Pot Muffins 72

Ho-Ho Cupcakes with
Cannabis Cream Filling 75

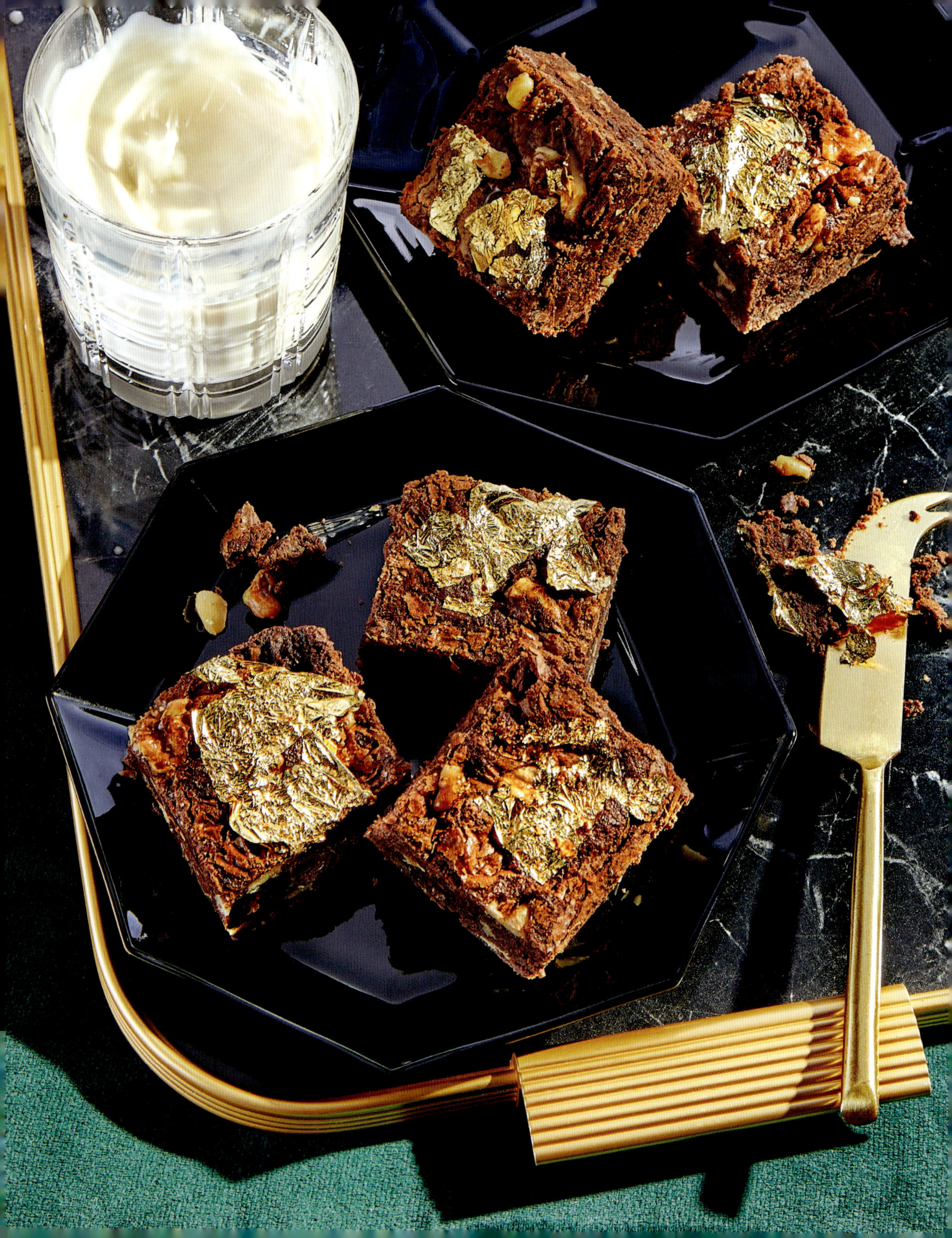

DANK DOUBLE-CHOCOLATE BROWNIES

- **MAKES ONE 9 BY 9 IN [23 BY 23 CM] PAN (20 BROWNIES)**
- **SERVING SIZE: 1 BROWNIE**
- **DOSAGE PER SERVING: FEELIN' GOOD (5 TO 6 MG THC); FOR SKY HIGH (10 TO 12 MG) USE 14 TBSP UNSALTED BUTTER AND 2 TBSP CANNABUTTER**
- **FOR VIRGIN (0 MG) USE 16 TBSP UNSALTED BUTTER ONLY**

1 cup [120 g] roughly chopped walnuts (optional)

8 oz [230 g] semisweet chocolate, roughly chopped

15 Tbsp [205 g] unsalted butter, cubed

1 Tbsp Cannabutter (page 15)

1 cup [140 g] all-purpose flour

1½ tsp kosher salt

⅔ cup [50 g] unsweetened Dutch-process cocoa powder

1⅔ cups [330 g] sugar

4 large eggs

1 cup [180 g] milk chocolate chips

¾ tsp flaky sea salt

Edible gold leaf, to garnish (optional)

CONTINUED ➡

BROWNIES, BLONDIES, AND MUFFINS

1. Preheat the oven to 350°F [180°C]. Spray a 9 by 9 in [23 by 23 cm] baking dish with cooking spray.

2. Spread the walnuts, if using, on a baking sheet lined with parchment paper or a silicone baking mat and toast until fragrant and starting to glisten, 10 minutes. Cool to room temperature.

3. In a medium saucepan, bring 3 in [7.5 cm] of water to a boil. Turn the heat down to medium-low and place a large heatproof bowl over the pan, making sure it does not touch the water. Place the semisweet chocolate, unsalted butter, and cannabutter in the bowl and, stirring occasionally, melt them together. Remove the bowl from the heat and let the mixture cool to room temperature.

4. Sift the flour, cocoa powder, and kosher salt together into a medium bowl.

5. In the bowl of a stand mixer fitted with the paddle attachment or in a medium bowl with a handheld electric mixer on high speed, cream the sugar and eggs until pale and bubbly.

6. With a spatula or wooden spoon, gently fold the sugar mixture into the chocolate mixture, scraping the bottom of the bowl to fully combine. Fold in the flour mixture until just combined, then fold in the chocolate chips and walnuts, if using.

7. Pour the batter into the prepared pan, spreading the mixture into the corners and smoothing the top with a spatula.

8. Bake until the sides are beginning to pull away from the pan and the center is no longer wobbly, about 35 minutes. Sprinkle with the flaky sea salt.

9. Place the pan on a wire rack and cool the brownies to room temperature, about 1 hour. Bling that sh*t out with gold leaf, if using. Then chill in the refrigerator for 1 hour or leave at room temperature, covered in plastic wrap, overnight to set.

10. Run a knife around the edges to loosen the brownies, then cut them into 20 portions. The brownies will keep, wrapped tightly with plastic wrap, on the countertop for up to 5 days or in the freezer for up to 1 month.

PEPPERMINT POT BROWNIES

- **MAKES ONE 9 BY 9 IN [23 BY 23 CM] PAN (20 BROWNIES)**
- **SERVING SIZE: 1 BROWNIE**
- **DOSAGE PER SERVING: FEELIN' GOOD (5 TO 6 MG THC); FOR SKY HIGH (10 TO 12 MG) USE 14 TBSP UNSALTED BUTTER AND 2 TBSP CANNABUTTER**
- **FOR VIRGIN (0 MG) USE 16 TBSP UNSALTED BUTTER ONLY**

8 oz [230 g] bittersweet chocolate, roughly chopped

15 Tbsp [205 g] unsalted butter, cubed

1 Tbsp Cannabutter (page 15)

1 cup [140 g] all-purpose flour

⅔ cup [50 g] unsweetened Dutch-process cocoa powder

1⅔ cups [330 g] sugar

3 large eggs

12 oz [340 g] Junior Mints or YORK Peppermint Patties Miniatures

3 Tbsp crushed Starlight mints

CONTINUED ➜

1. Preheat the oven to 350°F [180°C]. Spray a 9 by 9 in [23 by 23 cm] baking dish with cooking spray.

2. In a medium saucepan, bring 3 in [7.5 cm] of water to a boil. Turn the heat down to medium-low and place a large heatproof bowl over the pan, making sure it does not touch the water. Place the chocolate, unsalted butter, and cannabutter in the bowl and, stirring occasionally, melt them together. Remove the bowl from the heat and let the mixture cool to room temperature.

3. Sift the flour and cocoa powder together into a medium bowl.

4. In the bowl of a stand mixer fitted with the paddle attachment or in a medium bowl with a handheld electric mixer on high speed, cream the sugar and eggs until pale and bubbly.

5. With a spatula or wooden spoon, gently fold the chocolate mixture into the sugar mixture, scraping the bottom of the bowl to fully combine. Fold in the flour mixture until just combined, then fold in the Junior Mints.

6. Pour the batter into the prepared pan, spreading the mixture into the corners and smoothing the top with a spatula.

7. Bake until the sides are beginning to pull away from the pan and the center is no longer wobbly, about 35 minutes. Sprinkle the Starlight mints evenly over the top.

8. Place the pan on a wire rack and cool the brownies to room temperature, about 1 hour. Then chill in the refrigerator for 1 hour or leave at room temperature, covered in plastic wrap, overnight to set.

9. Run a knife around the edges to loosen the brownies, then cut them into 20 portions. The brownies will keep, wrapped tightly with plastic wrap, on the countertop for 5 days or in the freezer for up to 1 month.

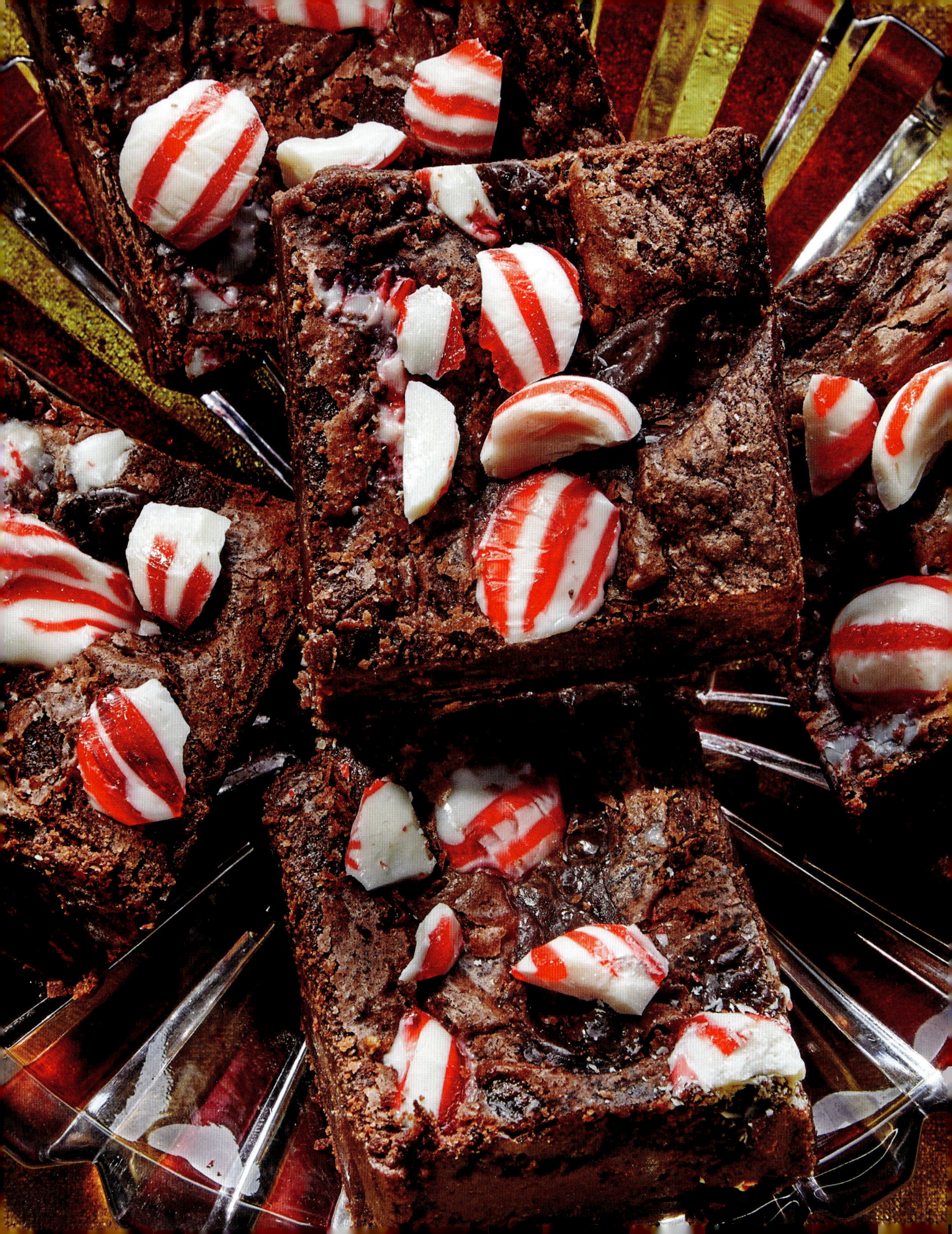

LOADED BROWN-BUTTER BLONDIES

- ◆ MAKES ONE 9 BY 9 IN [23 BY 23 CM] PAN (20 BLONDIES)
- ◆ SERVING SIZE: 1 BLONDIE
- ◆ DOSAGE PER SERVING: FEELIN' GOOD (5 TO 6 MG THC); FOR SKY HIGH (10 TO 12 MG) USE 14 TBSP UNSALTED BUTTER AND 2 TBSP CANNABUTTER
- ◆ FOR VIRGIN (0 MG) USE 16 TBSP UNSALTED BUTTER ONLY

15 Tbsp [205 g] unsalted butter, cubed

1 Tbsp Cannabutter (page 15)

2 cups [280 g] all-purpose flour

1 tsp kosher salt

1¾ cups [350 g] packed dark brown sugar

2 large eggs

4 tsp vanilla extract

⅔ cup [120 g] white chocolate chips

⅔ cup [95 g] chopped candied pineapple

⅔ cup [80 g] chopped macadamia nuts (optional)

1 tsp flaky sea salt

1. Preheat the oven to 350°F [180°C]. Spray a 9 by 9 in [23 by 23 cm] baking dish with cooking spray.

2. In a small saucepan over medium-low heat, melt the unsalted butter, swirling the pan until it smells nutty and brown flecks form in the bottom of the pan, about 10 minutes. Pour the butter into a large bowl, add the cannabutter, and stir to melt. Cool the butters to room temperature, about 15 minutes.

3. Sift the flour and kosher salt together into a medium bowl.

4. In the bowl of a stand mixer fitted with the paddle attachment or in a medium bowl with a handheld electric mixer on high speed, cream the sugar and eggs until pale and bubbly.

5. With a spatula or wooden spoon, gently fold the butter mixture and the vanilla into the egg mixture, scraping the bottom of the bowl to fully combine. Fold in the flour mixture until just combined. Fold in the white chocolate chips, pineapple, and macadamia nuts, if using.

6. Transfer the batter to the prepared pan, spreading it into the corners and smoothing the top with a spatula.

7. Bake the blondies for 40 minutes, until the top is starting to crack, the sides are beginning pull away from the pan, and the center is no longer wobbly. Sprinkle with the flaky sea salt.

8. Place the pan on a wire rack and cool the blondies to room temperature, about 1 hour. Then chill in the refrigerator for 1 hour or leave at room temperature, covered in plastic wrap, overnight to set.

9. Run a knife around the edges to loosen the blondies, then cut them into 20 portions. The blondies will keep, wrapped tightly with plastic wrap, on the countertop for 5 days or in the freezer for up to 1 month.

LOADED BROWN-BUTTER BLONDIES

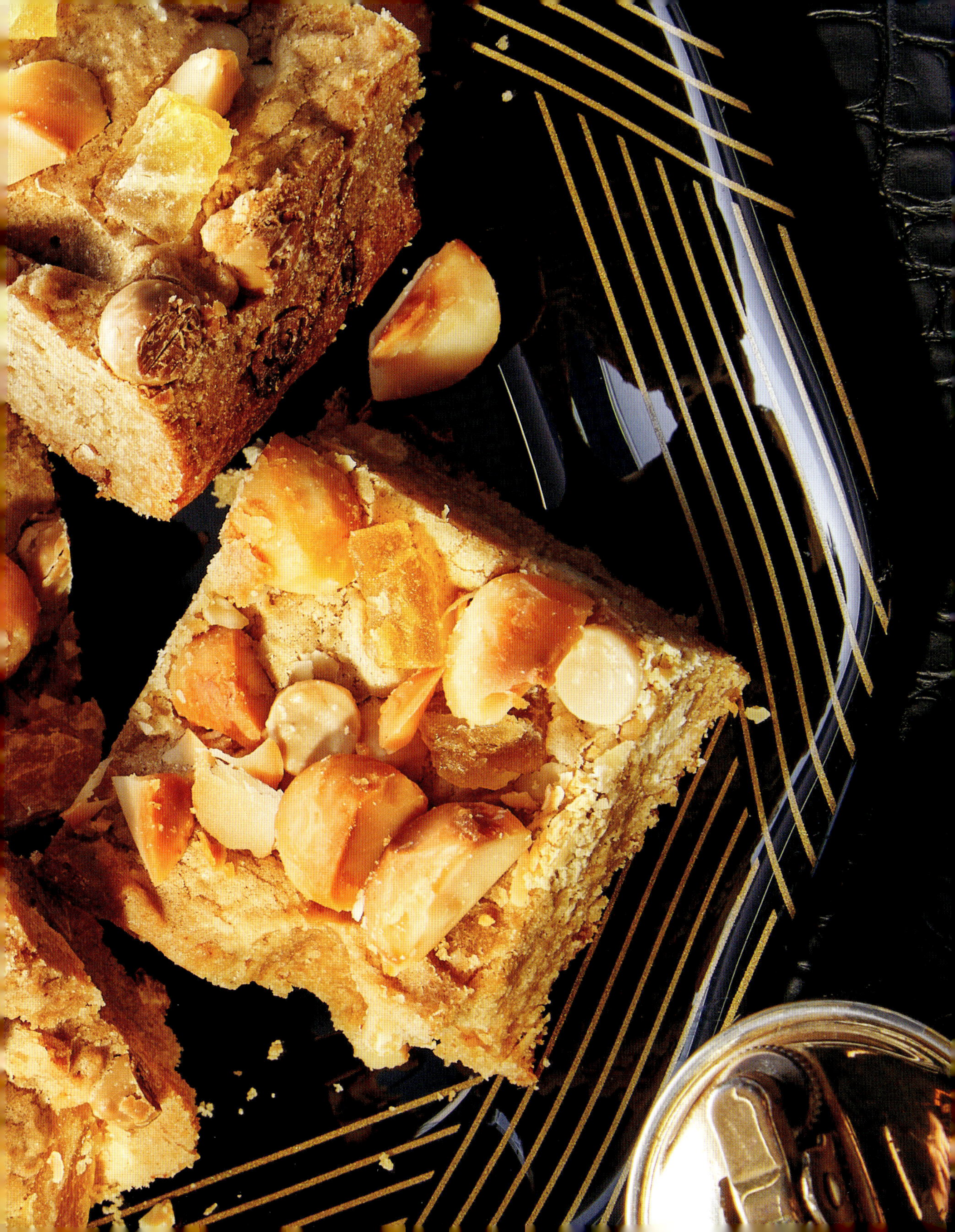

FRUIT LOOPS BARS WITH BENEFITS

- ✦ **MAKES ONE 9 BY 13 IN [23 BY 33 CM] PAN (24 BARS)**
- ✦ **SERVING SIZE: 1 BAR**
- ✦ **DOSAGE PER SERVING: FEELIN' GOOD (5 TO 6 MG THC); FOR SKY HIGH (10 TO 12 MG) USE 4 TBSP UNSALTED BUTTER AND 2 TBSP CANNABUTTER**
- ✦ **FOR VIRGIN (0 MG) USE 6 TBSP UNSALTED BUTTER ONLY**

5 Tbsp [75 g] unsalted butter

1 Tbsp Cannabutter (page 15)

1 lb [455 g] marshmallows

2 tsp vanilla extract

4 cups [100 g] crisped rice cereal

2½ cups [75 g] fruit loops or other colorful cereal

1 cup [180 g] white chocolate chips (optional)

1. Spray a 9 by 13 in [23 by 33 cm] baking pan with cooking spray. Spray a 9 by 13 in [23 by 33 cm] sheet of parchment paper with cooking spray.

2. In a large saucepan over medium heat, melt the butters together, stirring to combine. Add the marshmallows and stir until melted and smooth. Remove the saucepan from the heat and add the vanilla.

3. With a rubber or silicone spatula, quickly mix the crisped rice cereal, fruit loops, and white chocolate chips (if using) into the marshmallow mixture. Scoop the mixture into the prepared pan. Use the prepared parchment paper to firmly press the mixture into an even layer, filling the pan to the edges. Discard the parchment. Let the mixture sit at room temperature until cool, about 1 hour.

4. Turn the slab onto a cutting board, then cut it into 24 portions. The bars will keep, in an airtight container at room temperature, for up to 3 days.

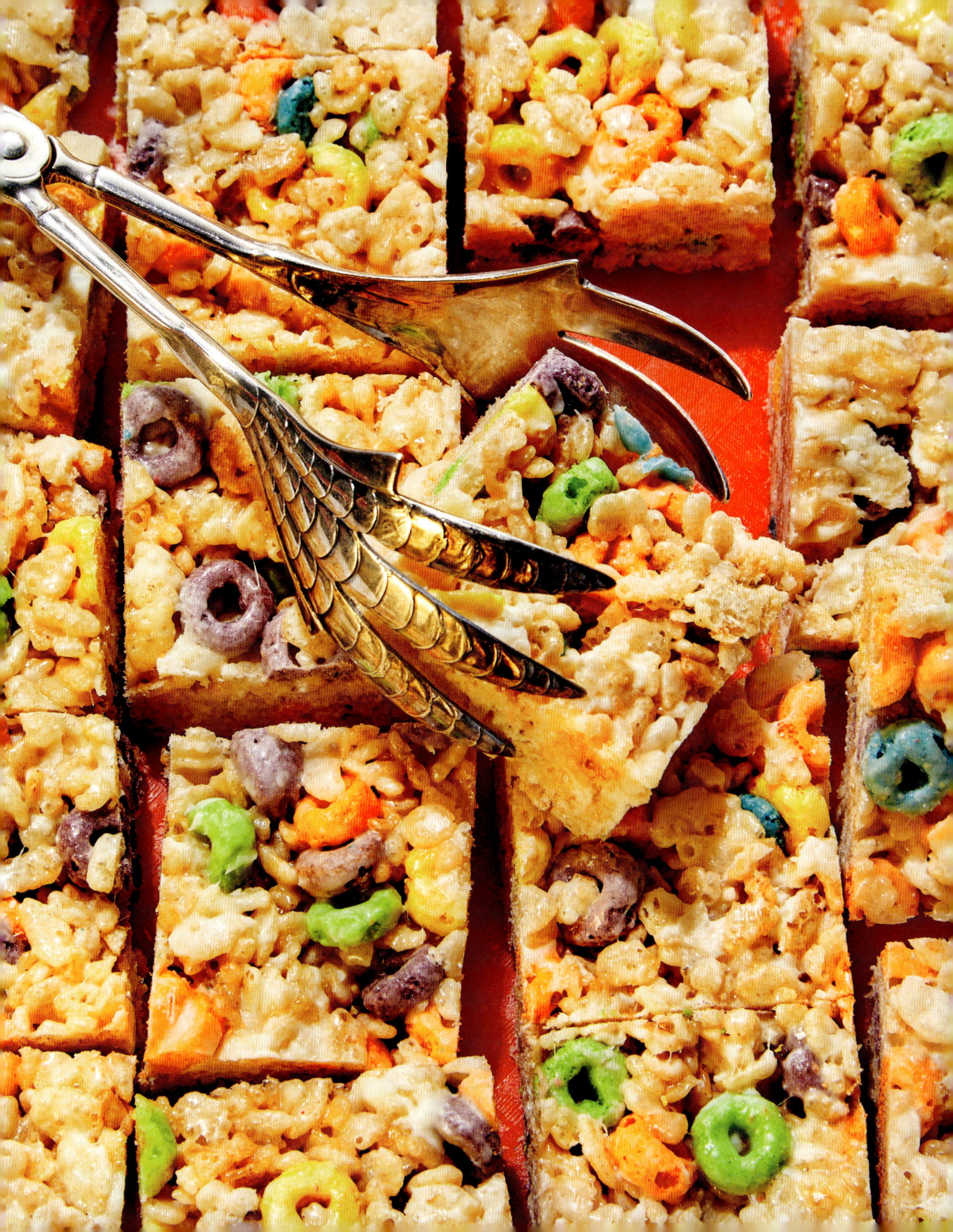

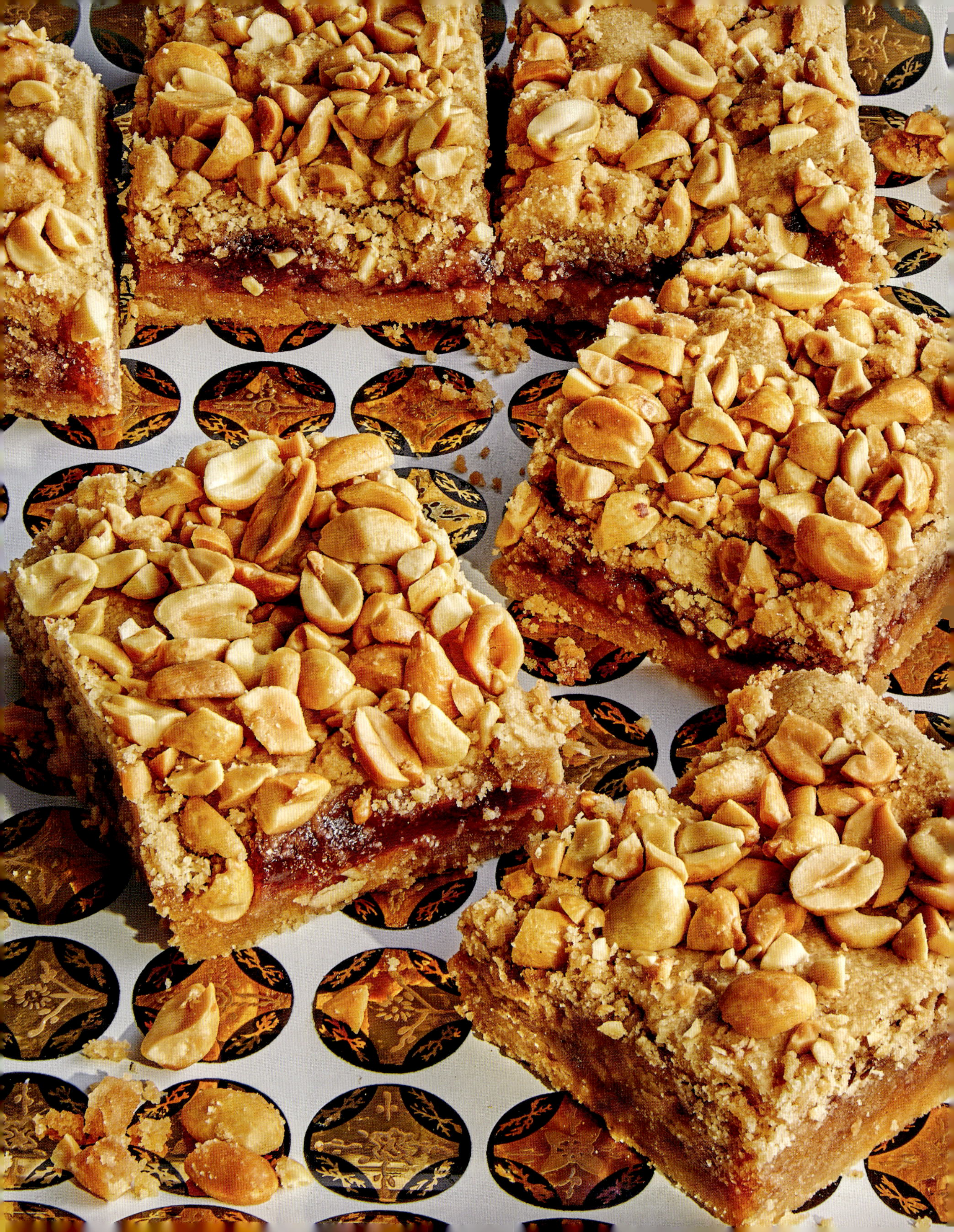

PB, C, AND J BARS

- **MAKES ONE 9 BY 13 IN [23 BY 33 CM] PAN (20 BARS)**
- **SERVING SIZE: 1 BAR**
- **DOSAGE PER SERVING: FEELIN' GOOD (5 TO 6 MG THC); FOR SKY HIGH (10 TO 12 MG) USE 10 TBSP UNSALTED BUTTER AND 2 TBSP CANNABUTTER**
- **FOR VIRGIN (0 MG) USE 12 TBSP UNSALTED BUTTER ONLY**

2¼ cups [315 g] all-purpose flour

1½ tsp kosher salt

¾ tsp baking powder

1 cup [200 g] sugar

11 Tbsp [155 g] unsalted butter, at room temperature

1 Tbsp Cannabutter (page 15)

1½ cups [390 g] creamy peanut butter

1 large egg

¾ tsp vanilla extract

2 cups [600 g] strawberry or raspberry jam

¾ cup [105 g] roasted, salted peanuts, roughly chopped

CONTINUED →

BROWNIES, BLONDIES, AND MUFFINS

1. Preheat the oven to 350°F [180°C]. Spray a 9 by 13 in [23 by 33 cm] baking pan with cooking spray.

2. In a medium bowl, whisk together the flour, salt, and baking powder.

3. In the bowl of a stand mixer fitted with the paddle attachment or in a medium bowl with a handheld electric mixer on high speed, cream the sugar, unsalted butter, and cannabutter until fluffy.

4. Lower the speed to medium-low and beat in the peanut butter, egg, and vanilla. Beat in the flour mixture until just combined into a crumbly dough.

5. Spread a third of the dough evenly in the prepared baking pan, pressing it into the corners and leveling the top with a spatula. Spread half the jam evenly over the top. Spread another third of the dough over the jam and top with the remaining jam. Spoon the remaining dough over the top and spread on the nuts.

6. Bake until golden brown, bubbling, and fragrant, 45 minutes to 1 hour. Cool to room temperature, run a knife around the edges to loosen the bars, and cut into 20 equal servings.

7. The bars will keep, wrapped tightly with plastic wrap, at room temperature for up to 5 days or in the freezer for up to 1 month.

PUMPKIN POT MUFFINS

- **MAKES 12 MUFFINS**
- **SERVING SIZE: 1 MUFFIN**
- **DOSAGE PER SERVING: FEELIN' GOOD (5 TO 6 MG THC); FOR SKY HIGH (10 TO 12 MG) USE 6 TBSP UNSALTED BUTTER AND 4 TSP CANNABIS OIL***
- **FOR VIRGIN (0 MG) USE 7 TBSP PLUS 2 TSP VEGETABLE OIL ONLY**

1¾ cups [245 g] all-purpose flour

¾ cup [150 g] packed light brown sugar

1 tsp baking soda

1 tsp ground cinnamon

1 tsp ground ginger

¾ tsp kosher salt

¼ tsp ground allspice

¼ tsp ground cloves

¼ tsp ground nutmeg

One 15 oz [430 g] can pumpkin purée

2 large eggs

7 Tbsp [105 ml] vegetable oil

2 tsp Cannabis Oil (page 15)

1 tsp vanilla extract

¾ cup [180 ml] Pourable Cream Cheese Frosting (page 24) or 1 cup [240 ml] Vanilla Buttercream Frosting (page 20) (optional)

CONTINUED →

BROWNIES, BLONDIES, AND MUFFINS

1. Preheat the oven to 400°F [200°C]. Line a 12-cup muffin tin with muffin liners or spray with cooking spray.

2. In a medium bowl, whisk together the flour, sugar, baking soda, cinnamon, ginger, salt, allspice, cloves, and nutmeg.

3. In another medium bowl, whisk together the pumpkin, eggs, vegetable oil, cannabis oil, and vanilla. Stir in the flour mixture to form a smooth, sticky batter.

4. Scoop ½ cup [120 g] of batter into each prepared cup and bake, rotating the muffin tin 180 degrees halfway through, until the muffins are golden brown and a cake tester inserted into the middle comes out clean, about 25 minutes.

5. Cool the muffins in the tin for 5 minutes. If you're going to frost them, transfer the muffins to a wire rack and let them cool fully before frosting. The muffins will keep in an airtight container at room temperature for up to 4 days or frozen for up to 1 month.

---

*Note: Swap out cannabis oil for vegetable oil and dose these cookies with dosed Pourable Cream Cheese Frosting (page 24) or Vanilla Buttercream Frosting (page 20) for the same dosage per serving. Using cannabis oil and a dosed frosting will double your dose.

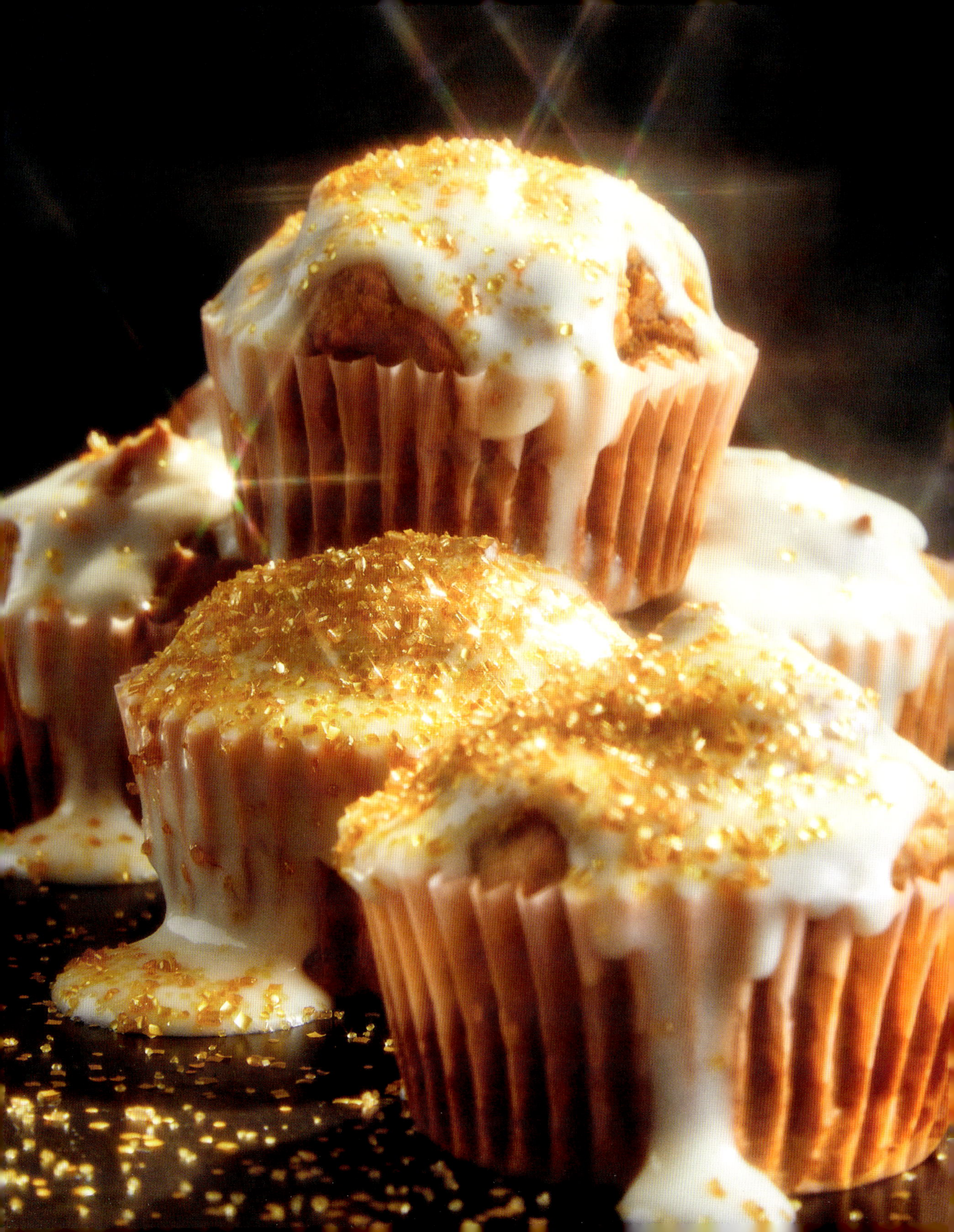

Lemon Poppy Seed Pot Muffins

- **MAKES 12 MUFFINS**
- **SERVING SIZE: 1 MUFFIN**
- **DOSAGE PER SERVING: FEELIN' GOOD (5 TO 6 MG THC); FOR SKY HIGH (10 TO 12 MG) USE 6 TBSP UNSALTED BUTTER AND 4 TSP CANNABUTTER***
- **FOR VIRGIN (0 MG) USE 7 TBSP PLUS 2 TSP UNSALTED BUTTER ONLY**

2½ cups [350 g] all-purpose flour

1½ tsp baking powder

½ tsp baking soda

¾ tsp kosher salt

¾ cup [150 g] sugar

1 cup [240 ml] whole milk

½ cup [120 g] sour cream

7 Tbsp [100 g] unsalted butter, melted and slightly cooled

2 tsp Cannabutter (page 15), at room temperature

2 large eggs

Zest of 2 lemons

¼ cup [60 ml] lemon juice

2 Tbsp poppy seeds

Lemon Glaze (page 26), for drizzling (optional)

CONTINUED →

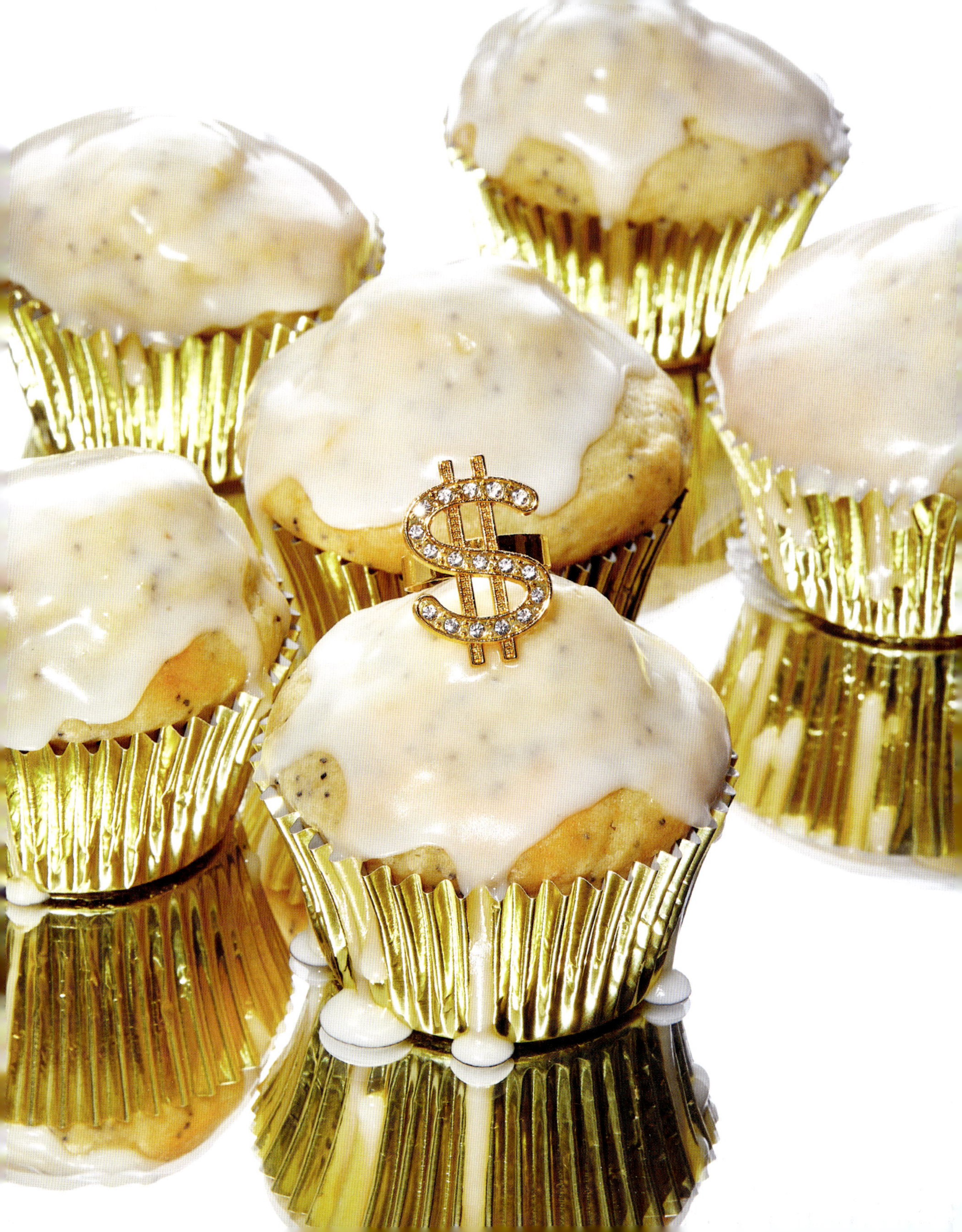

1. Preheat the oven to 350°F [180°C]. Line a 12-cup muffin tin with muffin liners or spray with cooking spray.

2. In a medium bowl, whisk together the flour, baking powder, baking soda, and salt.

3. In another medium bowl, stir together the sugar, milk, sour cream, unsalted butter, cannabutter, eggs, lemon zest, lemon juice, and poppy seeds. Stir in the flour mixture to form a smooth batter.

4. Scoop ½ cup [120 g] of batter into each prepared cup and bake, rotating the muffin tin 180 degrees halfway through, until the muffins are slightly golden and a cake tester inserted into the middle comes out clean, about 20 minutes.

5. Cool the muffins in the tin for 5 minutes. If you're going to frost them, transfer the muffins to a wire rack and let them cool fully before frosting. The muffins will keep in an airtight container at room temperature for 4 days or frozen for up to 1 month.

---

*Note: Swap out cannabutter for unsalted butter and dose these cookies with dosed Lemon Glaze (page 26) for the same dosage per serving. Using cannabutter and dosed glaze will double your dose.

HO-HO CUPCAKES WITH CANNABIS CREAM FILLING

- **MAKES 9 CUPCAKES**
- **SERVING SIZE: 1 CUPCAKE**
- **DOSAGE PER SERVING: FEELIN' GOOD (5 TO 6 MG THC); FOR SKY HIGH (10 TO 12 MG) USE 2 TBSP UNSALTED BUTTER AND 4 TSP CANNABUTTER**
- **FOR VIRGIN (0 MG) USE 3 TBSP PLUS 2 TSP UNSALTED BUTTER ONLY**

FOR THE CUPCAKES

¾ cup [105 g] all-purpose flour

¾ cup [150 g] granulated sugar

6 Tbsp [30 g] unsweetened Dutch-process cocoa powder, preferably black

¾ tsp baking soda

¾ tsp kosher salt

½ tsp baking powder

6 Tbsp [90 ml] buttermilk, at room temperature

¼ cup [60 ml] canola oil

1 large egg, at room temperature

1 tsp vanilla extract

6 Tbsp [90 ml] hot cocoa or hot water

FOR THE GANACHE

4 oz [115 g] bittersweet chocolate

½ cup [120 ml] heavy cream

FOR THE FILLING

3 Tbsp [25 g] confectioners' sugar

3 Tbsp [40 g] unsalted butter, at room temperature

2 tsp Cannabutter (page 15)

1½ cups [160 g] marshmallow fluff

FOR THE ICING

½ cup [50 g] confectioners' sugar

4 Tbsp unsalted butter, at room temperature

1½ Tbsp buttermilk

¼ tsp vanilla extract

CONTINUED →

TO MAKE THE CUPCAKES

1. Preheat the oven to 350°F [180°C]. Line a 12-cup muffin tin with muffin liners.

2. In a medium bowl, whisk together the flour, granulated sugar, cocoa powder, baking soda, salt, and baking powder. In another medium bowl, whisk together the buttermilk, oil, egg, and vanilla.

3. Make a well in the flour mixture and pour in the buttermilk mixture. Add the hot cocoa and stir the batter until smooth and well combined.

4. Fill the muffin liners two-thirds full with batter. Bake the cupcakes until a cake tester inserted into the middle comes out clean, about 30 minutes. Cool them in the pan until you can handle them, about 15 minutes, then transfer them to a wire rack to cool fully, about 1 hour.

TO MAKE THE GANACHE

1. In a medium saucepan, bring 3 in [7.5 cm] of water to a boil. Turn the heat down to medium-low and place a large heat-proof bowl over the saucepan, making sure it does not touch the water. Add the chocolate and cream to the bowl and, stirring, melt them together.

2. Remove the bowl from the heat and cool to room temperature, 15 minutes.

TO MAKE THE FILLING

1. In a medium bowl with a handheld electric mixer on low speed, cream the confectioners' sugar, unsalted butter, and cannabutter until fluffy. Beat in the marshmallow fluff until fully combined.

TO MAKE THE ICING

1. In a small bowl, cream the confectioners' sugar and butter together until fully combined. Beat in the buttermilk and vanilla until smooth.

TO FILL AND FROST THE CUPCAKES

1. Using a paring knife, cut a cone-shaped hole in the top of each cupcake. Remove the cut piece and slice off and discard all but the top ¼ in [6 mm] of it.

2. Fill a piping bag or a Ziploc bag with the filling and squeeze the air out, pushing the filling toward the tip or corner of the bag. Cut around the tip, or cut the corner off the Ziploc bag, and pipe 2 heaping Tbsp of the filling into the hole in each cupcake. Top the holes with the reserved pieces.

3. Spread the ganache on top of each cupcake. Fill another piping bag or a Ziploc bag with the icing and squeeze the air out, pushing the icing toward the tip or corner of the bag. Cut around the tip, or cut the corner off the Ziploc bag, and pipe a looping line of icing across the top of each cupcake.

4. The cupcakes will last in an airtight container in the refrigerator for up to 5 days.

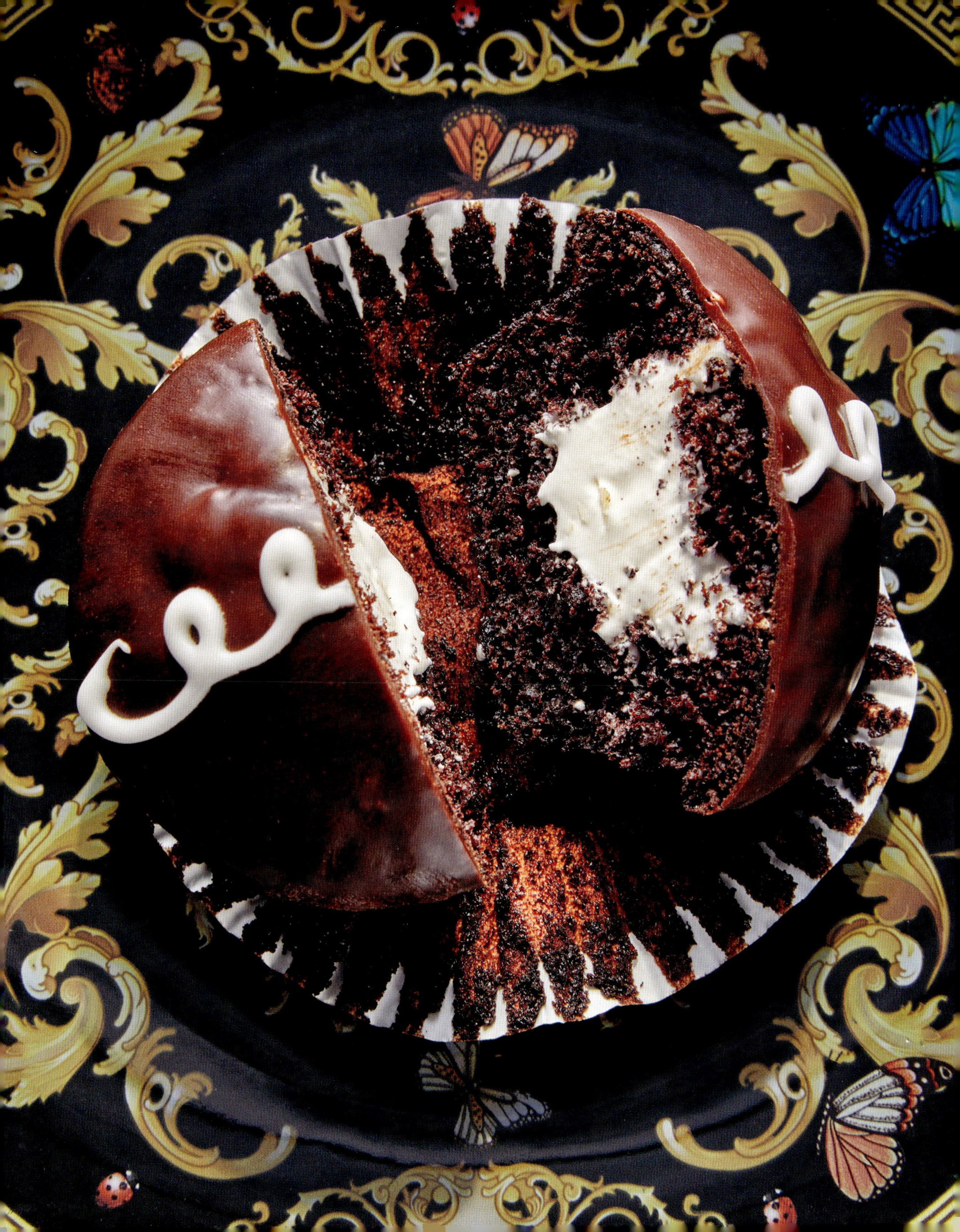

CAKES, PIES, AND PUDDINGS

Mellow Yellow Cake [80]

Red Velvet Blundt Cake [85]

Coconut Cannabis Cake [87]

Burnt Lil Cheesecakes [91]

The New 'Naner Bread [93]

Four Berries and a Bud Fruit Pie [96]

Mary Jane Pudding [101]

MELLOW YELLOW CAKE

- **MAKES ONE 9 IN [23 CM] LAYER CAKE (12 SLICES)**
- **SERVING SIZE: 1 SLICE**
- **DOSAGE PER SERVING: FEELIN' GOOD (5 TO 6 MG THC); FOR SKY HIGH (10 TO 12 MG) USE 10 TBSP UNSALTED BUTTER AND 4 TSP CANNABUTTER***
- **FOR VIRGIN (0 MG) USE 12 TBSP UNSALTED BUTTER ONLY**

3 cups [360 g] cake flour

1 Tbsp baking powder

¾ tsp kosher salt

1 cup [240 ml] buttermilk, at room temperature

2 tsp vanilla extract

2 cups [400 g] sugar

11 Tbsp [155 g] unsalted butter, at room temperature

2 tsp Cannabutter (page 15)

4 large eggs, at room temperature

2 cups [480 ml] Super-Fudgy Frosting (page 22) or Vanilla Buttercream Frosting (page 20)*

1. Preheat the oven to 350°F [180°C]. Spray two 9 in [23 cm] round cake pans with cooking spray.

2. In a medium bowl, sift together the flour, baking powder, and salt. In a small bowl, whisk together the buttermilk and vanilla.

3. In a stand mixer fitted with the paddle attachment or in a medium bowl with a handheld electric mixer on medium speed, beat the sugar, unsalted butter, and cannabutter together until fluffy.

4. Beat in the eggs one at a time. Beat in the flour mixture, alternating with the buttermilk mixture, in three additions, until a smooth, thick batter forms.

5. Divide the batter between the prepared pans and bake until golden brown and a cake tester inserted into the middle comes out clean, 30 to 35 minutes.

6. Cool the cakes for 15 minutes in the pans, then run a knife around the edges, invert them onto a wire rack, and cool for another 20 minutes.

7. Place one cake right-side up on a plate or cake stand and, using an offset spatula or butter knife, spread one-third of the frosting over the top. Position the other cake upside down on top of the iced cake and spread the remaining frosting over the top and sides, covering the cake.

8. Let the frosting set, about 1 hour, before cutting the cake to serve. The cake will last, wrapped tightly with plastic wrap, on the countertop for 3 days.

---

*Note: Swap out cannabutter for unsalted butter and frost this cake with dosed Super-Fudgy Frosting (page 22) or Vanilla Buttercream Frosting (page 20) for the same dosage per serving. Using cannabutter and the dosed frosting will double your dose.

mellow yellow
·CAKE·

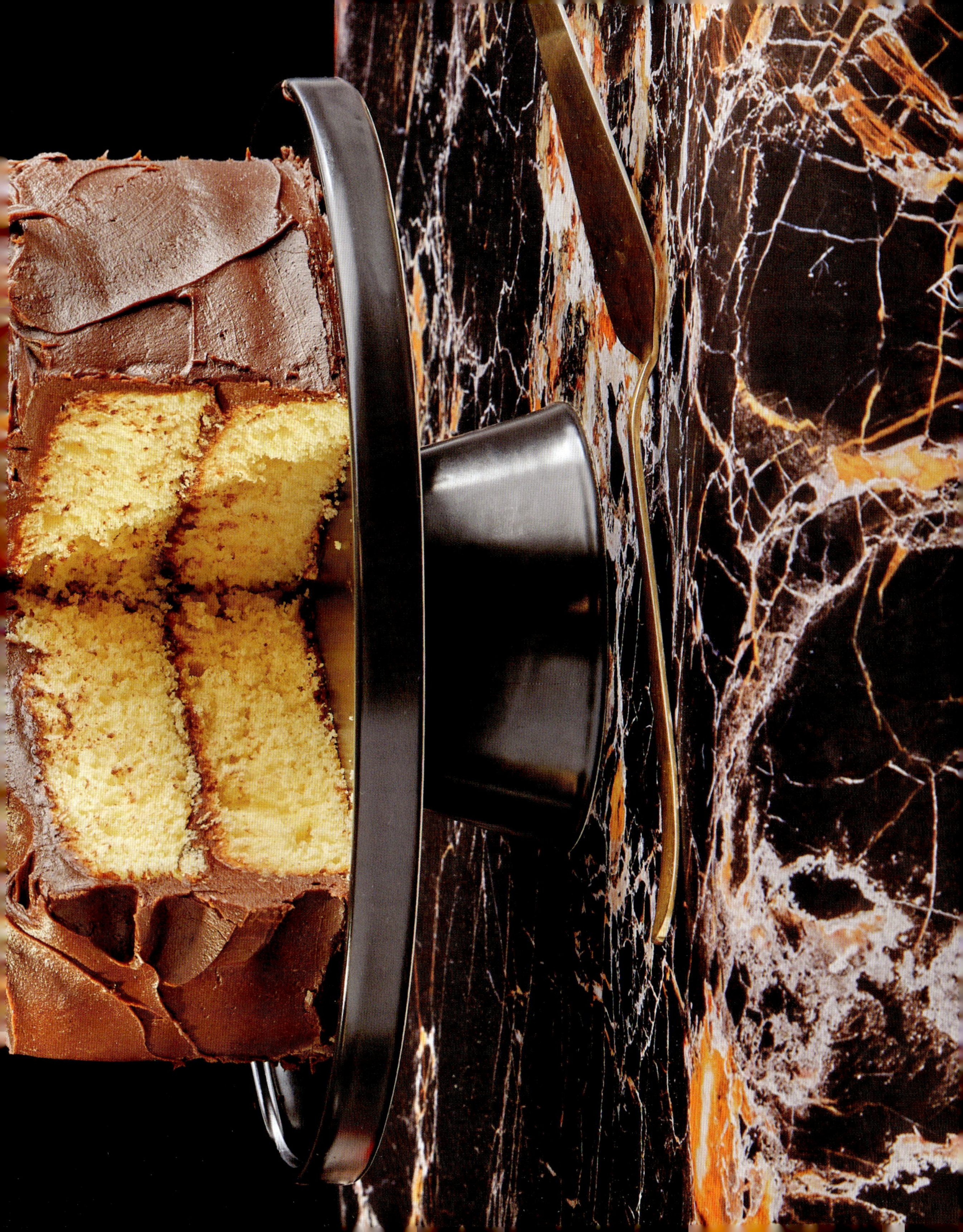

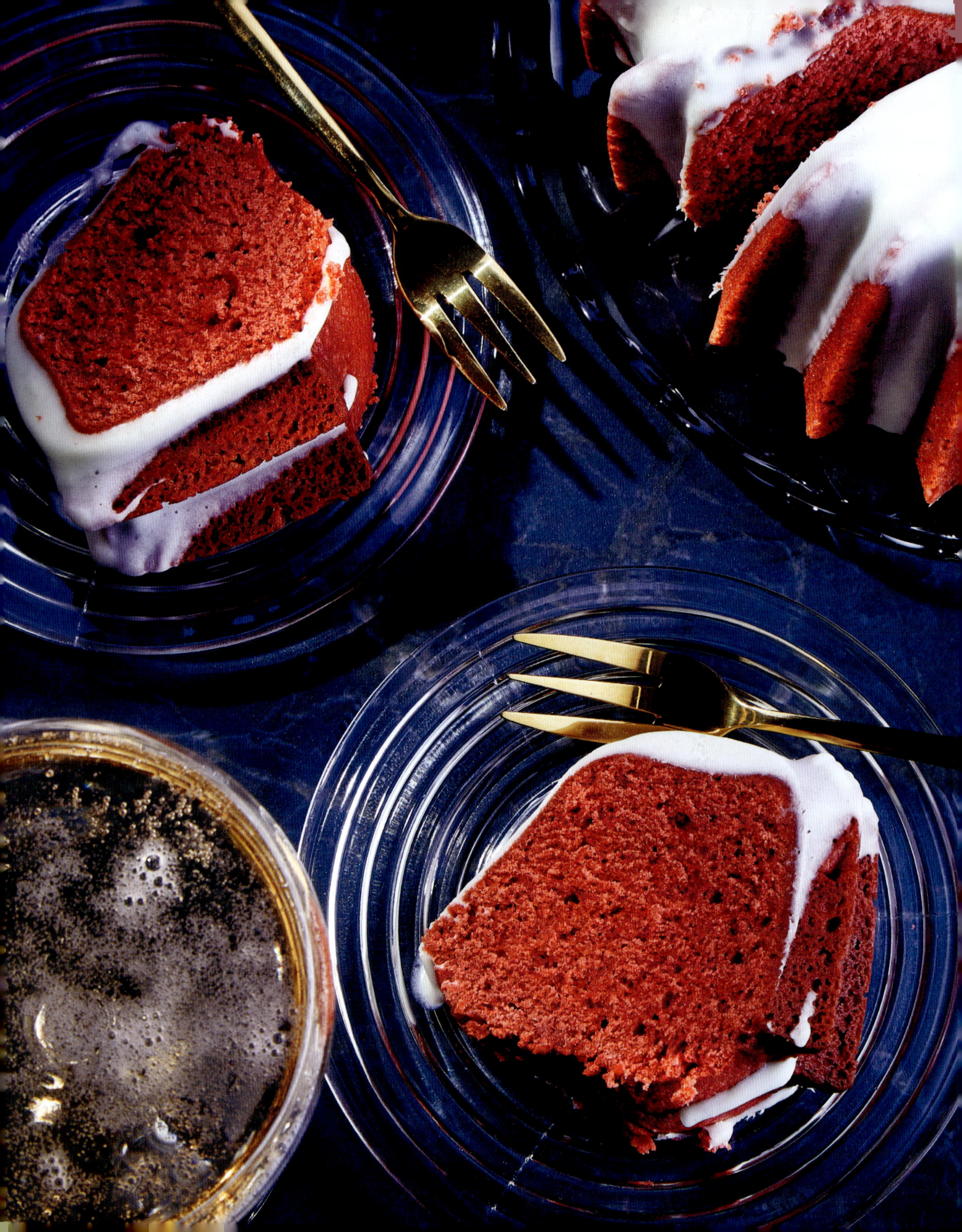

RED VELVET BLUNDT CAKE

- **MAKES ONE 9 IN [23 CM] BUNDT (16 SLICES)**
- **SERVING SIZE: 1 SLICE**
- **DOSAGE PER SERVING: FEELIN' GOOD (5 TO 6 MG THC); FOR SKY HIGH (10 TO 12 MG) USE 14 TBSP UNSALTED BUTTER AND 2 TBSP PLUS 1 TSP CANNABUTTER***
- **FOR VIRGIN (0 MG) USE 16 TBSP UNSALTED BUTTER ONLY**

2½ cups [350 g] all-purpose flour

2 Tbsp unsweetened cocoa powder

1 Tbsp baking powder

1 tsp kosher salt

1 cup [240 ml] buttermilk

1 Tbsp red food coloring

1 Tbsp distilled white vinegar

1 tsp vanilla extract

1½ cups [300 g] sugar

15 Tbsp [205 g] unsalted butter, at room temperature

2½ tsp Cannabutter (page 15), at room temperature

2 eggs

1 cup [240 ml] Pourable Cream Cheese Frosting (page 24)*

CONTINUED →

CAKES, PIES, AND PUDDINGS

1. Preheat the oven to 350°F [180°C]. Spray the inside of a 9 in [23 cm] Bundt pan with cooking spray.

2. In a medium bowl, sift together the flour, cocoa powder, baking powder, and salt. In another bowl, whisk together the buttermilk, food coloring, vinegar, and vanilla.

3. In the bowl of a stand mixer fitted with the paddle attachment or in a large bowl with an electric handheld mixer on medium speed, cream the sugar, unsalted butter, and cannabutter until fluffy, 3 to 5 minutes.

4. Beat in the eggs one at a time. Beat in a third of the flour mixture, alternating with the buttermilk mixture in three additions, to form a smooth, thick batter.

5. Transfer the batter to the prepared Bundt pan and drop the pan from 1 inch above the countertop to release air bubbles. Bake until a cake tester inserted into the middle comes out clean, 45 to 50 minutes.

6. Cool the cake for 15 minutes in the pan, invert it onto a wire rack, and cool for another 20 minutes.

7. Place the frosting in a pitcher-style measuring cup. Transfer the cake to a plate or cake stand and pour the frosting over the top of the cake, turning the cake as you pour so that frosting drips down the sides.

8. Let the frosting set, 15 minutes, then cut the cake into 16 slices to serve. The cake will last, wrapped tightly with plastic wrap, at room temperature for 3 days.

---

*Note: Swap out cannabutter for unsalted butter and frost this cake with a half recipe of dosed Pourable Cream Cheese Frosting (page 24) for the same dosage per serving. Using cannabutter and the dosed frosting will double your dose.

COCONUT CANNABIS CAKE

- **MAKES ONE 8 IN [20 CM] CAKE (12 SLICES)**
- **SERVING SIZE : 1 SLICE**
- **DOSAGE PER SERVING: FEELIN' GOOD (5 TO 6 MG THC); FOR SKY HIGH (10 TO 12 MG) USE ½ CUP PLUS 1 TBSP COCONUT OIL AND 1½ TBSP CANNABIS COCONUT OIL**
- **FOR VIRGIN (0 MG) USE 7 TBSP COCONUT OIL ONLY**

FOR THE CAKE

¾ cup [180 ml] unsweetened, full-fat coconut milk

2 cups [280 g] all-purpose flour

2½ tsp baking powder

¾ tsp kosher salt

1⅓ cups [265 g] granulated sugar

¾ cup [165 g] unrefined (virgin) coconut oil, at room temperature

2 tsp Cannabis Coconut Oil (page 15), at room temperature

½ tsp coconut extract

¼ tsp vanilla extract

3 large eggs, at room temperature

1 cup [80 g] unsweetened shredded coconut

FOR THE FROSTING

5 cups [500 g] confectioners' sugar

½ cup [110 g] unrefined (virgin) coconut oil, at room temperature

⅓ cup [80 ml] unsweetened, full-fat coconut milk

3 Tbsp coconut cream

1 tsp vanilla extract

2 cups [160 g] unsweetened shredded coconut

CONTINUED →

TO MAKE THE CAKE

1. Preheat the oven to 350°F [180°C]. Spray two 8 in [20 cm] cake pans with cooking spray.

2. Open the can of coconut milk and skim 3 Tbsp of coconut cream off the top to reserve for the frosting. Whisk the remaining cream and the milk in the can until fully combined. In a medium bowl, sift the flour, baking powder, and salt together.

3. In the bowl of a stand mixer fitted with the paddle attachment or in a medium bowl with a handheld electric mixer on medium speed, beat the granulated sugar, coconut oil, cannabis coconut oil, coconut extract, and vanilla until combined.

4. Beat in the eggs one at a time. Beat in the flour mixture, alternating with the coconut milk, in three additions, until a smooth, thick batter forms. Fold in the shredded coconut.

5. Divide the batter between the prepared pans and bake until golden brown and a cake tester inserted into the middle comes out clean, 30 to 35 minutes. Cool the cakes for 15 minutes in the pans, then run a knife around the edges, invert the cakes onto a wire rack, and cool for another 20 minutes.

TO MAKE THE FROSTING AND FROST THE CAKE

1. In the bowl of a stand mixer fitted with the paddle attachment or in a food processor, beat the confectioners' sugar, coconut oil, coconut milk, coconut cream, and vanilla together to form a smooth frosting.

2. Place one cake right-side up on a plate or cake stand and, using an offset spatula or butter knife, spread one-third of the frosting over the top. Sprinkle with ¼ cup [20 g] of the shredded coconut.

3. Position the other cake upside down on top of the iced cake and spread the remaining frosting over the top and sides, covering the cake. Press the remaining shredded coconut onto the top and sides of the cake.

4. Let the frosting set, about 1 hour, before cutting the cake to serve. The cake will last, wrapped tightly with plastic wrap, on the countertop for 3 days.

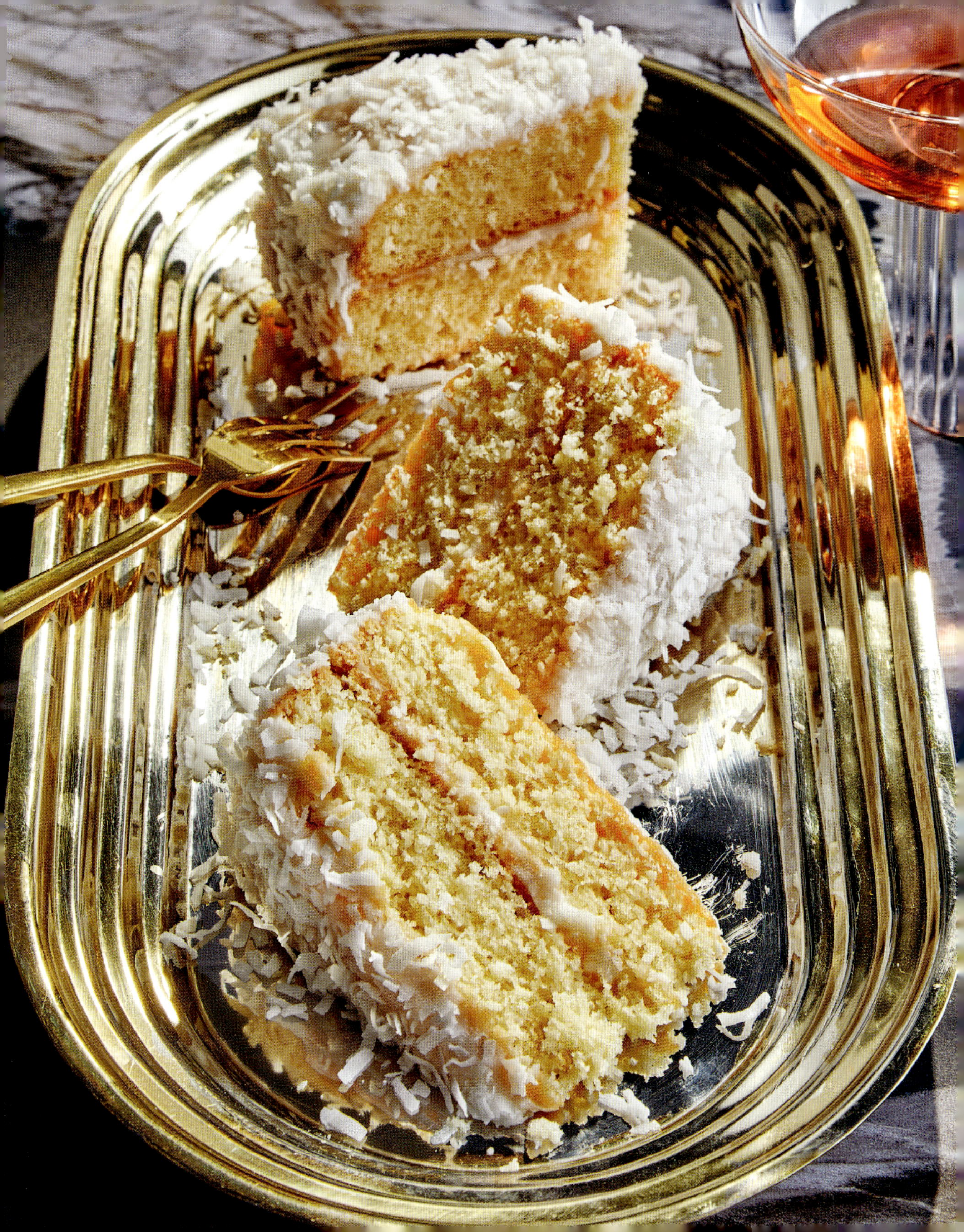

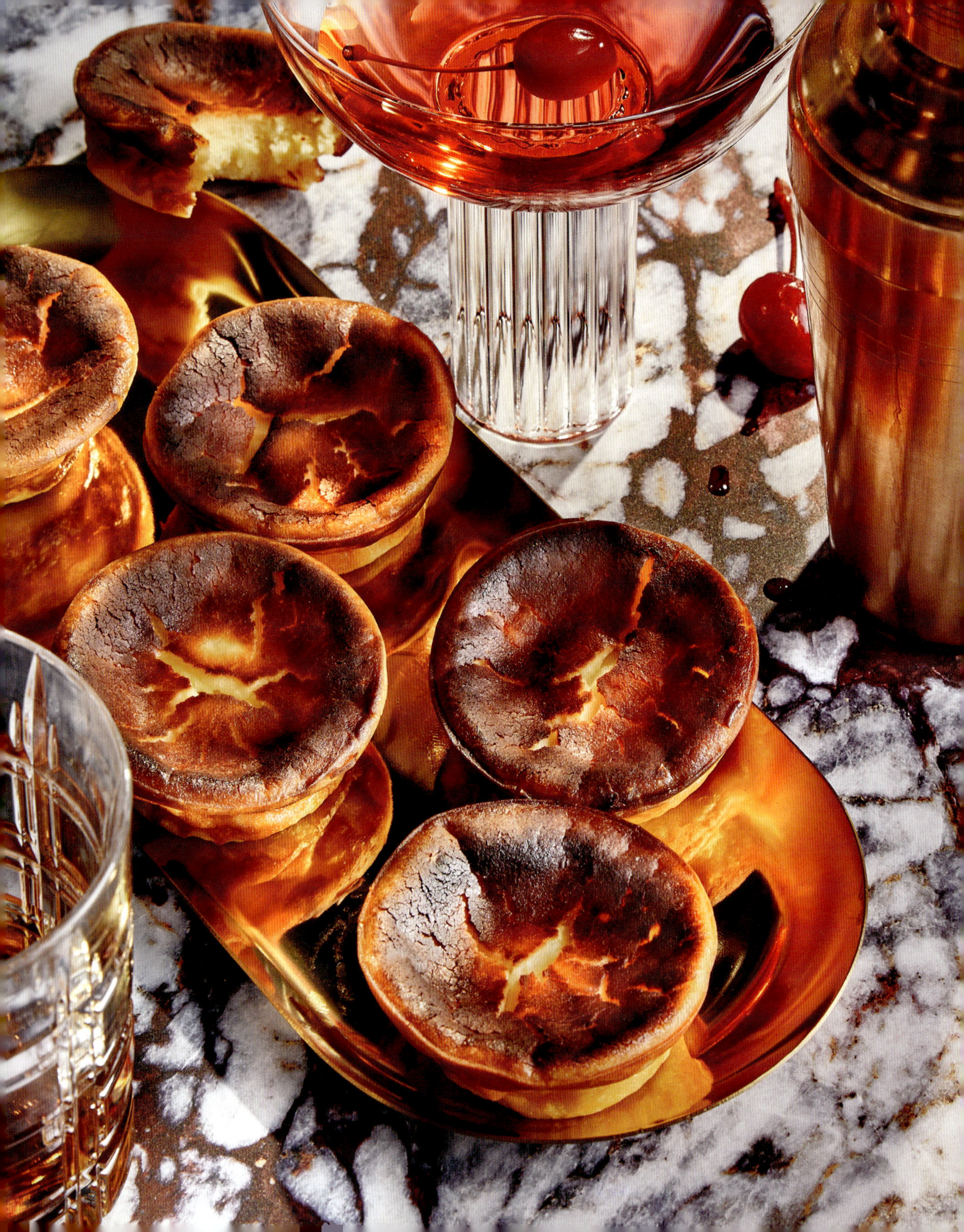

BURNT LIL CHEESECAKES

- **MAKES 12 CHEESECAKES**
- **SERVING SIZE: 1 CHEESECAKE**
- **DOSAGE PER SERVING: FEELIN' GOOD (5 TO 6 MG THC); FOR SKY HIGH (10 TO 12 MG) USE 4 TSP CANNABUTTER**
- **FOR VIRGIN (0 MG) SKIP CANNABUTTER**

2 lb [910 g] cream cheese, at room temperature

¾ cup [150 g] granulated sugar

2 tsp Cannabutter (page 15)

3 large eggs, at room temperature

1 cup [240 ml] heavy cream

½ tsp vanilla extract

½ tsp kosher salt

2 Tbsp all-purpose flour

CONTINUED ➡

1. Preheat the oven to 400°F [200°C]. Set the top rack 6 in [15 cm] from the broiler. Line a 12-cup muffin tin with muffin liners or spray with cooking spray.

2. In the bowl of a stand mixer fitted with the paddle attachment or in a medium bowl with a handheld electric mixer on medium-low speed, beat the cream cheese, sugar, and cannabutter until fluffy.

3. Beat in the eggs one at a time. Beat in the heavy cream, vanilla, and salt. Sift in the flour and beat until a smooth batter forms.

4. Ladle the batter into the prepared muffin cups. Bake until still loose and jiggly in the middle, about 15 minutes. Turn on the broiler to low and broil until the tops are browned, 5 minutes more.

5. Let the cakes cool and collapse before removing them from the tin, about 20 minutes. The cheesecakes will last in an airtight container in the refrigerator for up to 1 week.

THE NEW 'NANER BREAD

- MAKES ONE 9 BY 5 IN [23 BY 13 CM] LOAF (6 SLICES)
- SERVING SIZE: 1 SLICE
- DOSAGE PER SERVING: FEELIN' GOOD (5 TO 6 MG THC); FOR SKY HIGH (10 TO 12 MG) USE 7 TBSP UNSALTED BUTTER AND 2 TSP CANNABUTTER
- FOR VIRGIN (0 MG) USE 8 TBSP UNSALTED BUTTER ONLY

FOR THE BREAD

8 Tbsp [110 g] unsalted butter

1 tsp Cannabutter (page 15)

1½ cups [210 g] all-purpose flour

½ cup [100 g] granulated sugar

½ cup [100 g] packed dark brown sugar

1 tsp ground cinnamon

1 tsp baking soda

½ tsp kosher salt

2 or 3 very ripe bananas

2 large eggs

¼ cup [85 g] honey or molasses

¼ cup [60 ml] whole milk

¾ cup [135 g] chocolate chips

FOR THE TOPPING

¼ cup [50 g] packed dark brown sugar

2 Tbsp granulated sugar

2 tsp ground cinnamon

¼ tsp kosher salt

CONTINUED →

CAKES, PIES, AND PUDDINGS

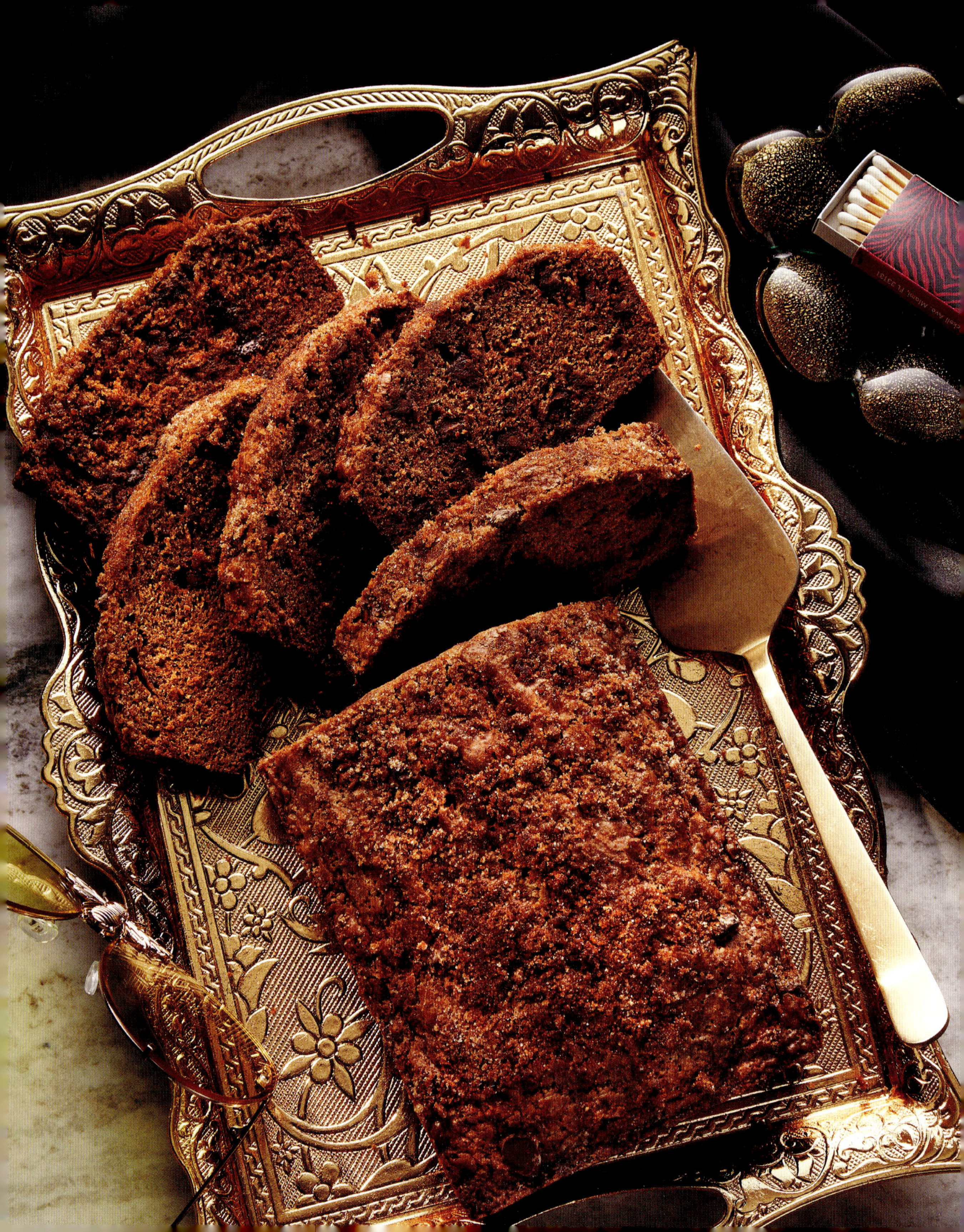

TO MAKE THE BREAD

1. Preheat the oven to 350°F [180°C]. Spray a 9 by 5 in [23 by 13 cm] loaf pan with cooking spray.

2. In a small saucepan over medium-low heat, melt the unsalted butter and cannabutter together, stirring to combine.

3. In a medium bowl, whisk together the flour, granulated sugar, brown sugar, cinnamon, baking soda, and salt.

4. In a large bowl with a fork, mash the bananas to a smooth paste. Whisk in the melted butters, eggs, honey, and milk until smooth. Add the flour mixture and stir until just combined. Stir in the chocolate chips. Pour the batter into the prepared pan.

TO MAKE THE TOPPING AND BAKE

1. In a small bowl, mix together the brown sugar, granulated sugar, cinnamon, and salt, using your fingers to break up any lumps. Sprinkle the mixture evenly over the batter.

2. Bake until a cake tester inserted into the middle of the bread comes out clean, about 1 hour. Cool for 30 minutes before removing the bread from the pan. Transfer to a wire rack to cool fully, about 30 minutes more, before slicing. The bread will last, wrapped tightly with plastic wrap, on the countertop for up to 3 days and in the freezer for up to 1 month.

FOUR BERRIES AND A BUD FRUIT PIE

- ◆ MAKES ONE 10 IN [25 CM] PIE (12 SLICES)
- ◆ SERVING SIZE: 1 SLICE
- ◆ DOSAGE PER SERVING: FEELIN' GOOD (5 TO 6 MG THC); FOR SKY HIGH (10 TO 12 MG) USE 12½ TBSP UNSALTED BUTTER AND 1½ TBSP CANNABUTTER
- ◆ FOR VIRGIN (0 MG) USE 14 TBSP PLUS 2 TSP UNSALTED BUTTER ONLY

FOR THE DOUGH

3 cups [420 g] all-purpose flour, plus more for dusting

14 Tbsp [190 g] unsalted butter, chilled and cubed

2 tsp Cannabutter (page 15)

2 tsp kosher salt

½ cup [120 ml] chilled water

FOR THE FILLING

1 lb [455 g] strawberries, hulled and roughly chopped

6 oz [170 g] blackberries

6 oz [170 g] blueberries

6 oz [170 g] raspberries

¾ cup [150 g] granulated sugar

3 Tbsp cornstarch

1 Tbsp lemon zest

1 tsp fresh lemon juice

½ tsp kosher salt

1 egg

TO MAKE THE DOUGH

1. In a food processor, pulse the flour, unsalted butter, cannabutter, and salt to a sandy consistency. Add the water and pulse just until a dough forms.

2. Divide the dough into two rough balls and flatten each into a disc. Wrap the discs tightly in plastic wrap and chill for 1 hour. The dough will keep, wrapped tightly, in the refrigerator overnight or in the freezer for up to 1 month.

3. On a lightly floured surface with a lightly floured rolling pin, roll out one disc of dough to about 12 in [30.5 cm]. Tuck it into a 10 in [25 cm] pie pan and trim the edges. Chill the dough while you make the filling and the lattice.

TO MAKE THE FILLING

1. In a medium saucepan over medium-high heat, bring the strawberries, blackberries, blueberries, raspberries, sugar, cornstarch, lemon zest, lemon juice, and salt to a simmer, stirring, until the berries start to break down, about 5 minutes. Lower the heat to medium-low and cook until the mixture thickens, about 25 minutes. Cool to room temperature, then pour into the chilled crust.

2. Preheat the oven to 400°F [200°C]. On a lightly floured surface with a lightly floured rolling pin, roll out the remaining disc of dough to about 12 in [30.5 cm] and cut the dough into 1½ in [4 cm] strips. Arrange the lattice strips on top of the pie, alternating them under and over, and trim the edges. (Or use a cannabis leaf cookie cutter to cut out shapes and place over the filling.)

3. Beat the egg with 1 Tbsp of water and brush the dough with it. Bake the pie until the crust is golden brown and the filling is bubbling, 40 to 45 minutes. If the crust is getting too dark before the filling bubbles, cover it loosely with aluminum foil.

4. Let the pie cool completely, about 1 hour, before slicing. The pie will last, wrapped tightly with plastic wrap, on the countertop overnight or in the refrigerator for up to 5 days.

FOUR BERRIES AND A BUD FRUIT PIE

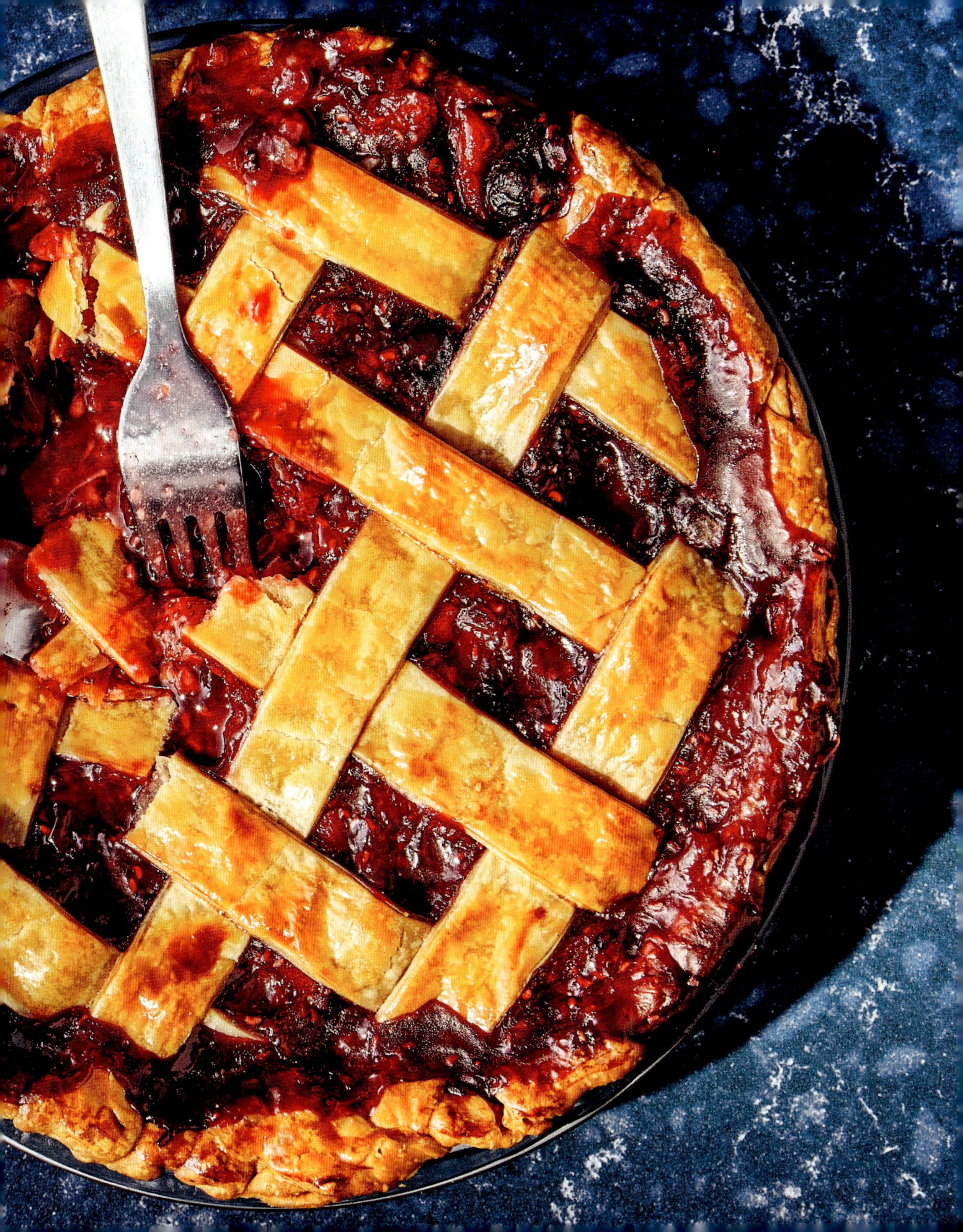

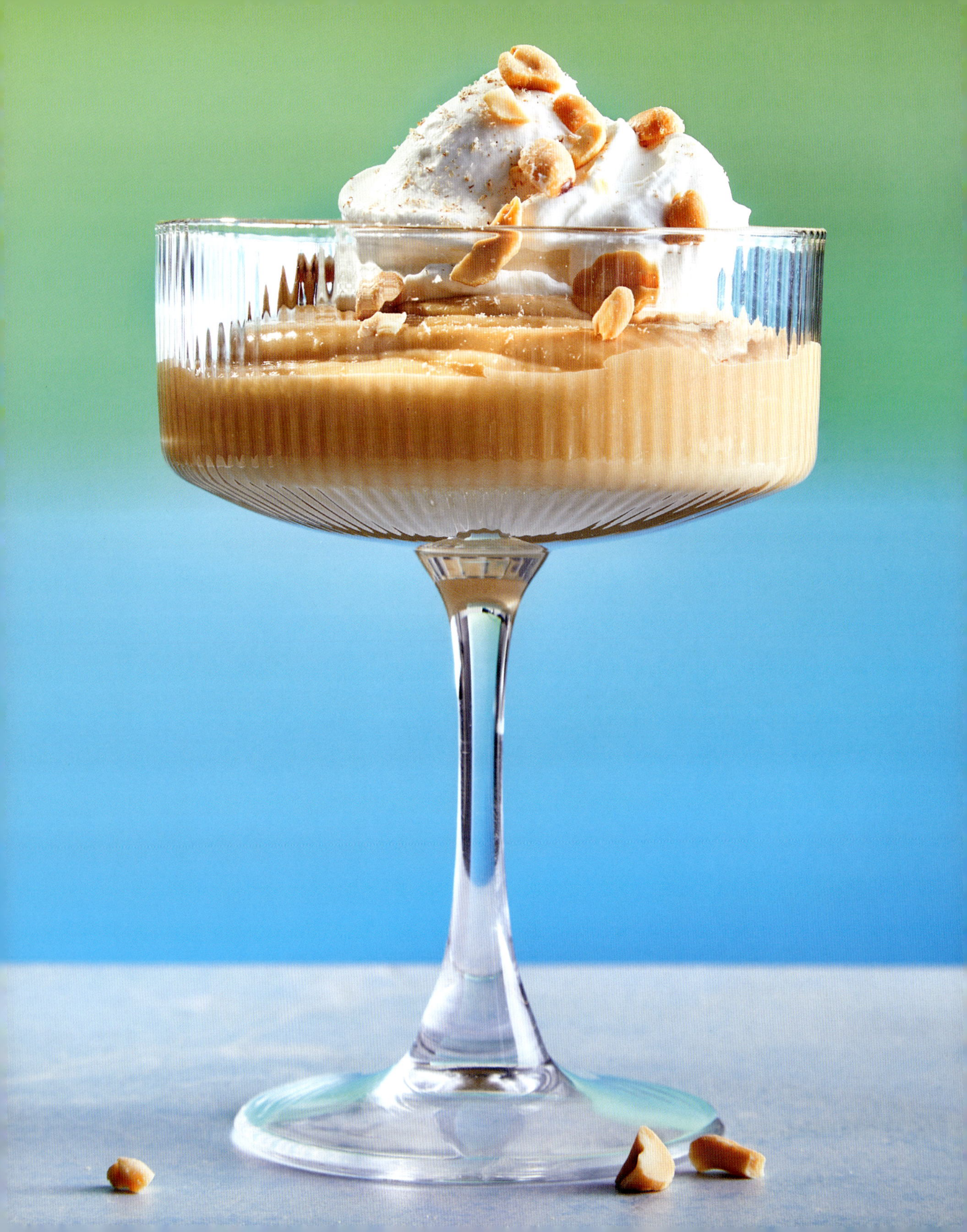

MARY JANE PUDDING

- **MAKES 8 PUDDINGS**
- **SERVING SIZE: 1 PUDDING**
- **DOSAGE PER SERVING: FEELIN' GOOD (5 TO 6 MG THC); FOR SKY HIGH (10 TO 12 MG) USE 1 TBSP UNSALTED BUTTER AND 1 TBSP CANNABUTTER**
- **FOR VIRGIN (0 MG) USE 2 TBSP UNSALTED BUTTER ONLY**

1½ cups [300 g] packed dark brown sugar

¼ cup [35 g] cornstarch

½ tsp kosher salt

2 cups [480 ml] whole milk

2 cups [480 ml] heavy cream

4 large egg yolks

1 Tbsp bourbon

2 tsp vanilla extract

1½ Tbsp unsalted butter, cubed

1¼ tsp Cannabutter (page 15)

Whole nutmeg, for garnish

Roasted salted peanuts, roughly chopped, for garnish

1. In a medium Dutch oven, whisk together the brown sugar, cornstarch, and salt. Whisk in the milk, 1 cup [240 ml] of the heavy cream, egg yolks, bourbon, and vanilla.

2. Cook over medium heat, whisking constantly, until the mixture thickens to pudding consistency, 8 to 10 minutes. Add the unsalted butter and cannabutter and whisk until they're melted and combined.

3. Remove the pudding from the heat and divide it among 8 small heatproof serving dishes or espresso cups. Chill for at least 1 hour and up to overnight.

4. In a tall jar using an immersion blender, whip the remaining 1 cup [240 ml] of cream until stiff peaks form, about 3 minutes. Top each pudding with some whipped cream, grate some nutmeg over the top, and sprinkle on some peanuts to serve. The pudding will last, wrapped tightly with plastic wrap, in the refrigerator for up to 3 days.

WAKE AND BAKES

with Hot Honey Cannabutter [117]

Bacon Cheddar Scallion Biscuits [120]

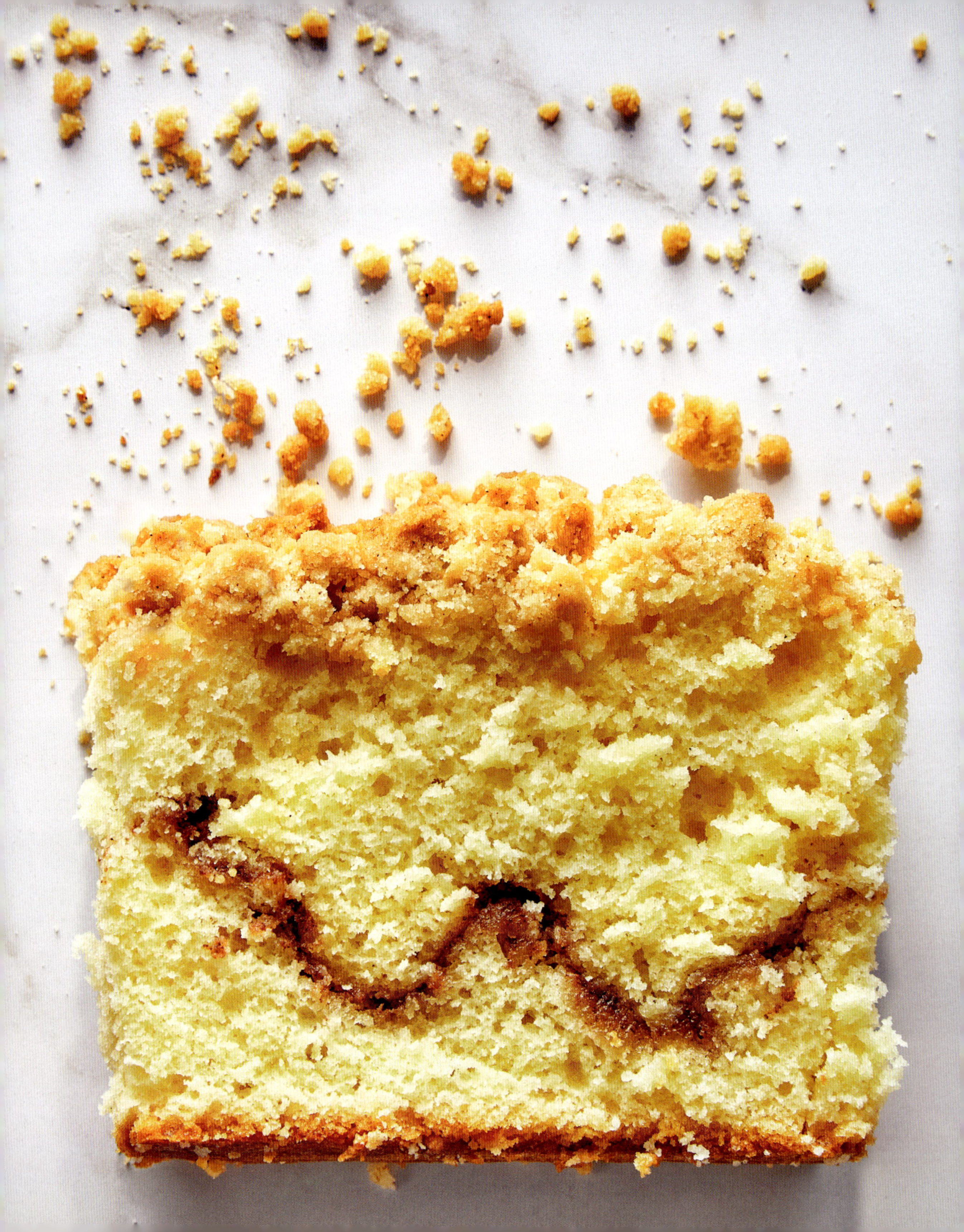

MORNING BUZZ COFFEE CAKE

- **MAKES ONE 9 BY 13 IN [23 BY 33 CM] CAKE (16 SLICES)**
- **SERVING SIZE: 1 SLICE**
- **DOSAGE PER SERVING: FEELIN' GOOD (5 TO 6 MG THC); FOR SKY HIGH (10 TO 12 MG) USE 15 TBSP UNSALTED BUTTER AND 2 TBSP CANNABUTTER**
- **FOR VIRGIN (0 MG) USE 16 TBSP UNSALTED BUTTER ONLY**

FOR THE STREUSEL

1 cup [200 g] packed brown sugar

1 cup [140 g] all-purpose flour

2 tsp ground cinnamon

Pinch of kosher salt

½ cup [110 g] unsalted butter, at room temperature

FOR THE FILLING

¼ cup [50 g] granulated sugar

1 Tbsp all-purpose flour

1 tsp ground cinnamon

FOR THE CAKE

3 cups [420 g] all-purpose flour

2¼ cups [450 g] granulated sugar

¾ tsp baking powder

½ tsp baking soda

½ tsp kosher salt

1 cup [220 g] unsalted butter, at room temperature

2½ tsp Cannabutter (page 15), at room temperature

1 cup [240 g] sour cream

¼ cup [60 ml] whole milk

4 large eggs

1 Tbsp vanilla extract

CONTINUED ➡

TO MAKE THE STREUSEL

1. In a small bowl, whisk together the brown sugar, flour, cinnamon, and salt. Using a fork or your hand, rub the butter into the mixture until it forms a crumbly topping.

TO MAKE THE FILLING

1. In a small bowl, whisk together the granulated sugar, flour, and cinnamon.

TO MAKE THE CAKE

1. Preheat the oven to 375°F [190°C] and spray a 9 by 13 in [23 by 33 cm] baking pan with cooking spray.

2. In a medium bowl, whisk together the flour, granulated sugar, baking powder, baking soda, and salt. Using a handheld electric mixer on medium-low speed, beat in the unsalted butter and cannabutter until the mixture is like wet sand.

3. In another medium bowl, whisk together the sour cream, milk, eggs, and vanilla until well combined and uniform. Add to the flour mixture and beat to form a smooth batter.

4. Spread half the batter evenly in the prepared pan, then sprinkle it evenly with the cinnamon sugar filling. Carefully spread the remaining batter evenly over the cinnamon sugar. Sprinkle the streusel evenly over the top.

5. Bake until a cake tester inserted into the middle comes out clean, about 1 hour. Cool in the pan to room temperature, about 1 hour, before cutting into 16 pieces. The cake will last, wrapped tightly with plastic wrap, at room temperature for up to 3 days.

MORNING GLOW MUFFINS

- **MAKES 18 MUFFINS**
- **SERVING SIZE: 1 MUFFIN**
- **DOSAGE PER SERVING: FEELIN' GOOD (5 TO 6 MG THC); FOR SKY HIGH (10 TO 12 MG) USE ¾ CUP PLUS 2 TBSP VEGETABLE OIL AND 2 TBSP CANNABIS OIL**
- **FOR VIRGIN (0 MG) USE ¾ CUP PLUS 4 TBSP VEGETABLE OIL ONLY**

1¼ cups [175 g] all-purpose flour

1¼ cups [175 g] whole wheat flour

¾ cup [150 g] packed light brown sugar

2 tsp ground cinnamon

1½ tsp baking soda

1 tsp kosher salt

¼ tsp baking powder

¼ tsp ground nutmeg

¼ tsp ground allspice

¼ tsp ground ginger

2 medium carrots, peeled and finely grated

1 apple, peeled, cored, and finely grated

½ cup [75 g] roughly chopped dates

½ cup [70 g] raisins

½ cup [70 g] roughly chopped dried, sweetened pineapple

½ cup [60 g] roughly chopped pecans

½ cup [40 g] shredded, unsweetened coconut

Zest of 1 orange

4 large eggs

¾ cup plus 3 Tbsp [225 ml] vegetable oil

1 Tbsp Cannabis Oil (page 15)

¼ cup [85 g] honey

CONTINUED →

1. Preheat the oven to 400°F [200°C]. Spray 18 muffin cups with cooking spray or line them with muffin liners.

2. In a medium bowl, whisk together the all-purpose flour, whole wheat flour, sugar, cinnamon, baking soda, salt, baking powder, nutmeg, allspice, and ginger.

3. In another medium bowl, toss together the carrots, apple, dates, raisins, pineapple, pecans, coconut, and orange zest. Stir in the eggs, vegetable oil, cannabis oil, and honey until combined. Fold in the flour mixture to form a chunky batter.

4. Scoop ½ cup [120 g] of batter into each prepared cup and bake, rotating the tins 180 degrees halfway through, until the muffins are deep brown and a cake tester inserted into the middle comes out clean, about 25 minutes.

5. Cool the muffins in the tin for 10 minutes. The muffins will keep in an airtight container at room temperature for up to 4 days or frozen for up to 1 month.

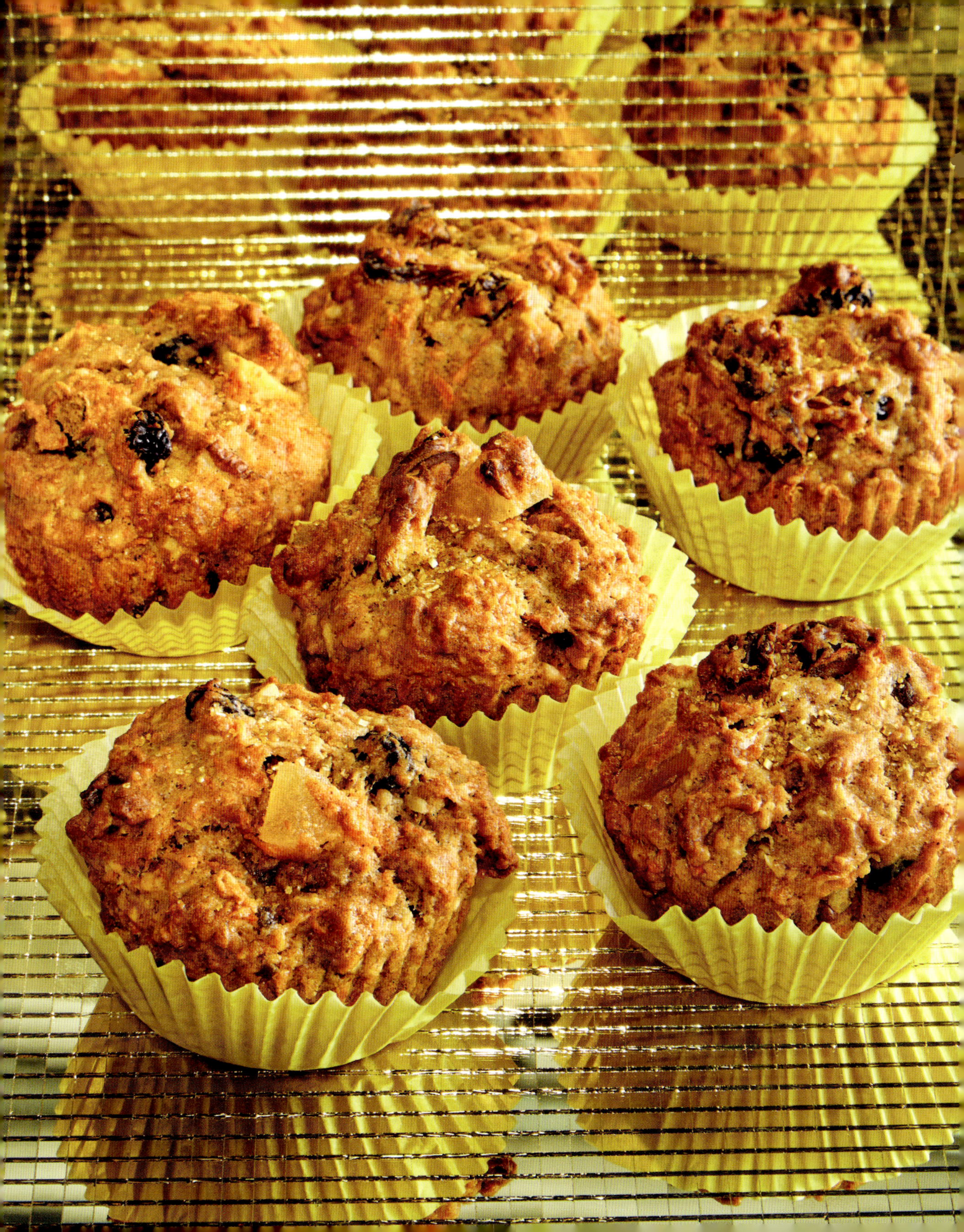

BUD-DERMILK PANCAKES WITH STONER SYRUP

- **MAKES 15 PANCAKES**
- **SERVING SIZE: 3 PANCAKES PLUS 2 TBSP SYRUP**
- **DOSAGE PER SERVING: FEELIN' GOOD (5 TO 6 MG THC); FOR SKY HIGH (10 TO 12 MG) USE ½ TSP CANNABIS GLYCERINE TINCTURE**
- **FOR VIRGIN (0 MG) SKIP CANNABIS GLYCERINE TINCTURE**

FOR THE MAPLE SYRUP

10 Tbsp [150 ml] maple syrup

¼ tsp Cannabis Glycerine Tincture (page 15)

FOR THE PANCAKES

2 cups [280 g] all-purpose flour

3 Tbsp granulated sugar

1½ tsp baking powder

1 tsp baking soda

1 tsp kosher salt

3 Tbsp unsalted butter

½ tsp Cannabutter (page 15)

2½ cups [600 ml] buttermilk

2 large eggs

TO MAKE THE MAPLE SYRUP

1. Pour the maple syrup into a small pitcher. Stir in the cannabis glycerine tincture, stirring for at least 2 minutes to evenly distribute the dose.

TO MAKE THE PANCAKES

1. Preheat the oven to 200°F [100°C]. Place a wire rack on a baking sheet in the oven.

2. In a large bowl, whisk together the flour, sugar, baking powder, baking soda, and salt.

3. In a small saucepan over medium-low heat, melt the unsalted butter and cannabutter together, stirring to combine.

4. Using a rubber spatula, scrape the butters into a medium bowl and whisk in the buttermilk and eggs. Add the flour mixture and stir to combine.

5. Spray a large, nonstick pan with cooking spray and heat it over medium-low heat until the oil is shimmering. Ladle the batter into the pan ⅓ cup [80 ml] at a time, making sure not to crowd the pan. Cook until air bubbles rise to the surface and the pancakes are golden brown on the bottom, 2 to 3 minutes. Flip and cook until golden brown on the other side, 1 to 2 minutes more.

6. Place pancakes on the prepared baking sheet in the oven to stay warm and re-spray the pan between batches. Place 3 pancakes on each plate and top with 2 Tbsp of syrup to serve. The pancakes will keep, in an airtight container in the refrigerator, for up to 5 days and in the freezer for up to 2 months. Reheat them in the microwave for 20 seconds each or wrapped in foil in a 350°F [180°C] oven for 10 minutes.

BUD-DERMILK PANCAKES

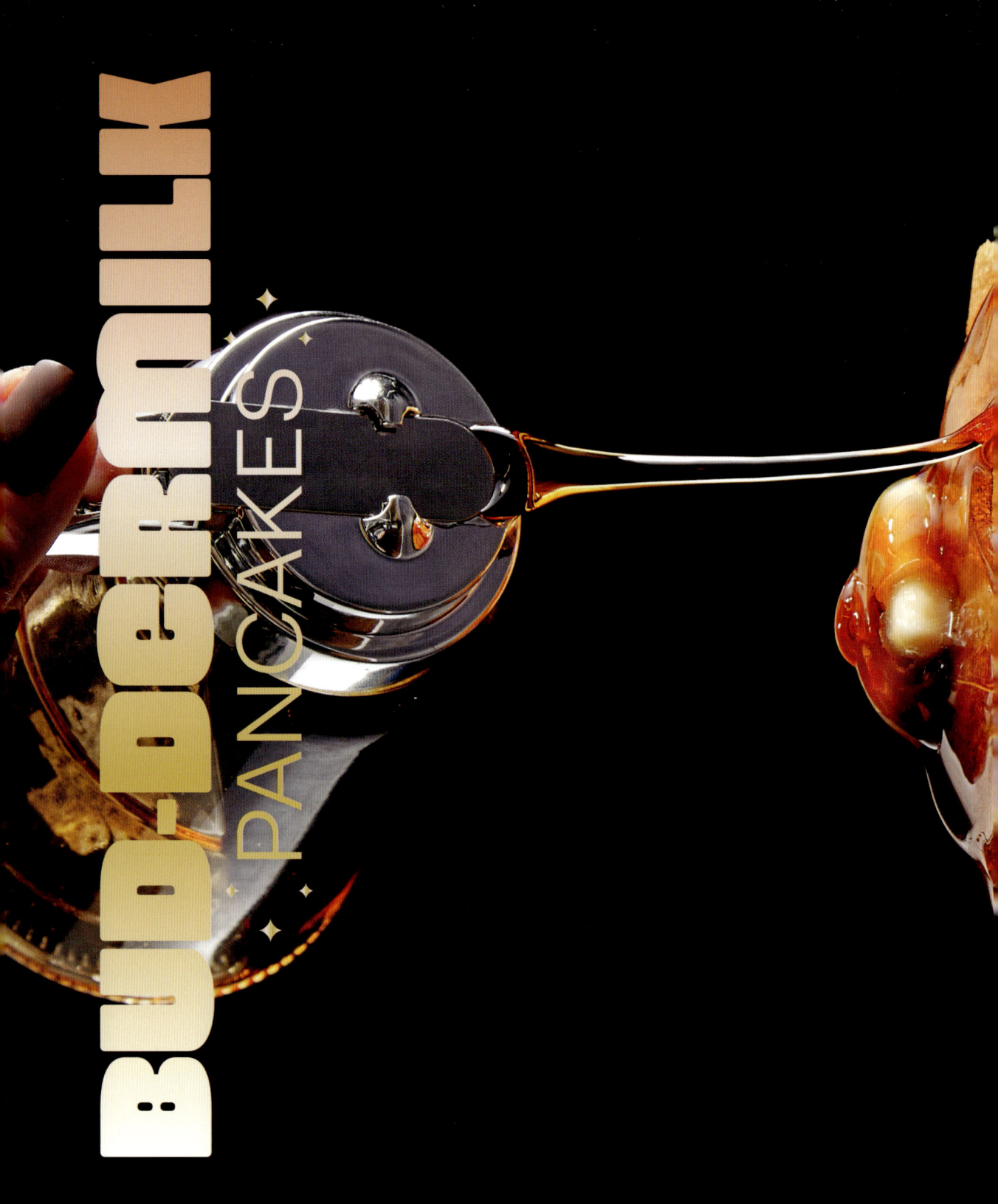

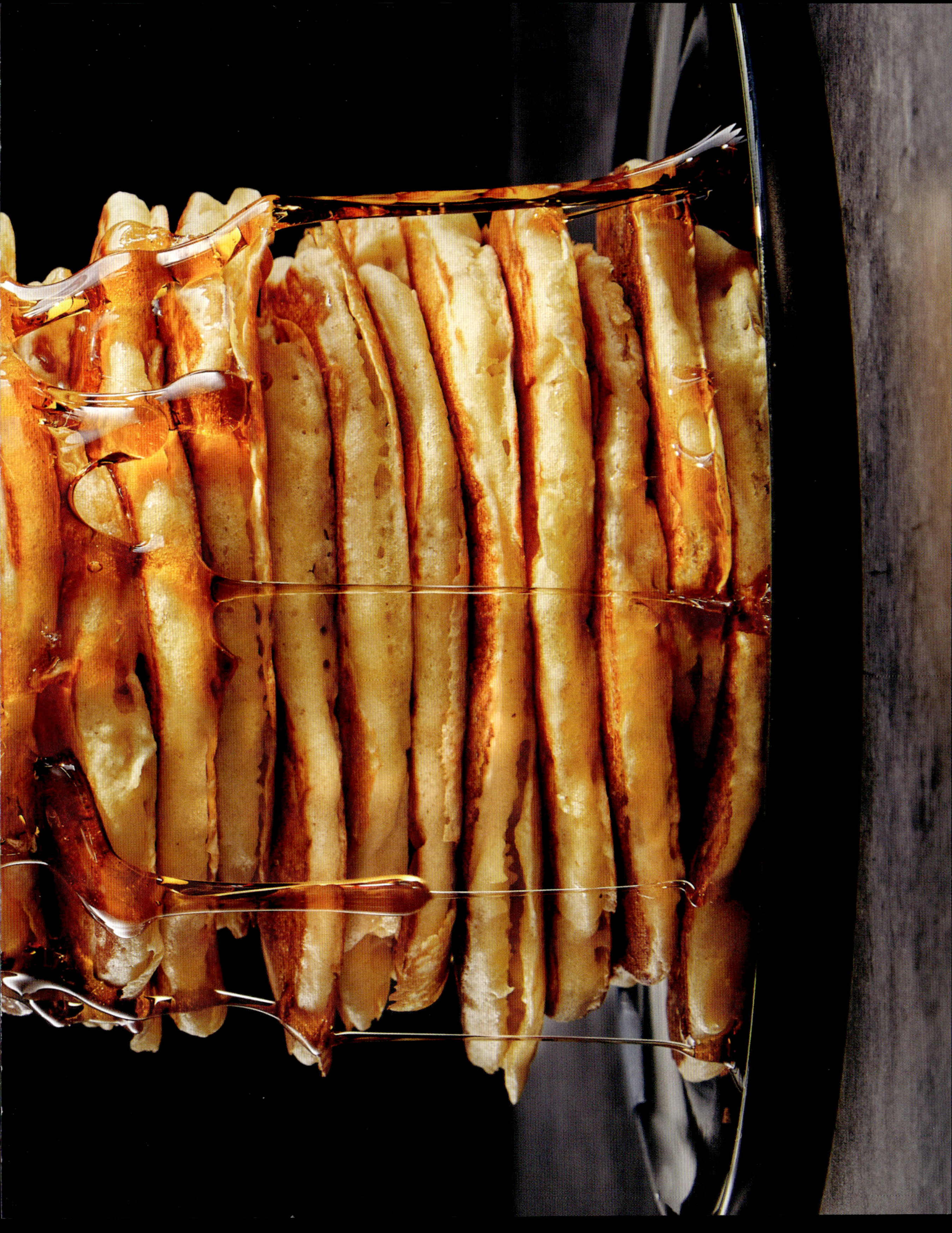

Whole Weed Waffles with Blueberry Cannabis Compote

- **MAKES 10 WAFFLES**
- **SERVING SIZE: 2 WAFFLES PLUS 6 TBSP COMPOTE**
- **DOSAGE PER SERVING: FEELIN' GOOD (5 TO 6 MG THC); FOR SKY HIGH (10 TO 12 MG) USE ½ TSP CANNABIS GLYCERINE TINCTURE IN COMPOTE AND 1 TSP CANNABUTTER IN WAFFLES**
- **FOR VIRGIN (0 MG) SKIP CANNABIS GLYCERINE TINCTURE AND CANNABUTTER**

FOR THE COMPOTE

1½ lb [680 g] blueberries

3 Tbsp granulated sugar

1 Tbsp lemon juice

¼ tsp Cannabis Glycerine Tincture or Cannabis Coconut Oil (page 15)

FOR THE WAFFLES

2 cups [280 g] whole wheat flour

1 Tbsp sugar

1 tsp kosher salt

1 tsp baking powder

½ tsp baking soda

5½ Tbsp [80 g] unsalted butter

½ tsp Cannabutter (page 15)

1 cup [240 g] sour cream

1 cup [240 ml] whole milk

4 large eggs

Lemon zest, to garnish

CONTINUED ➜

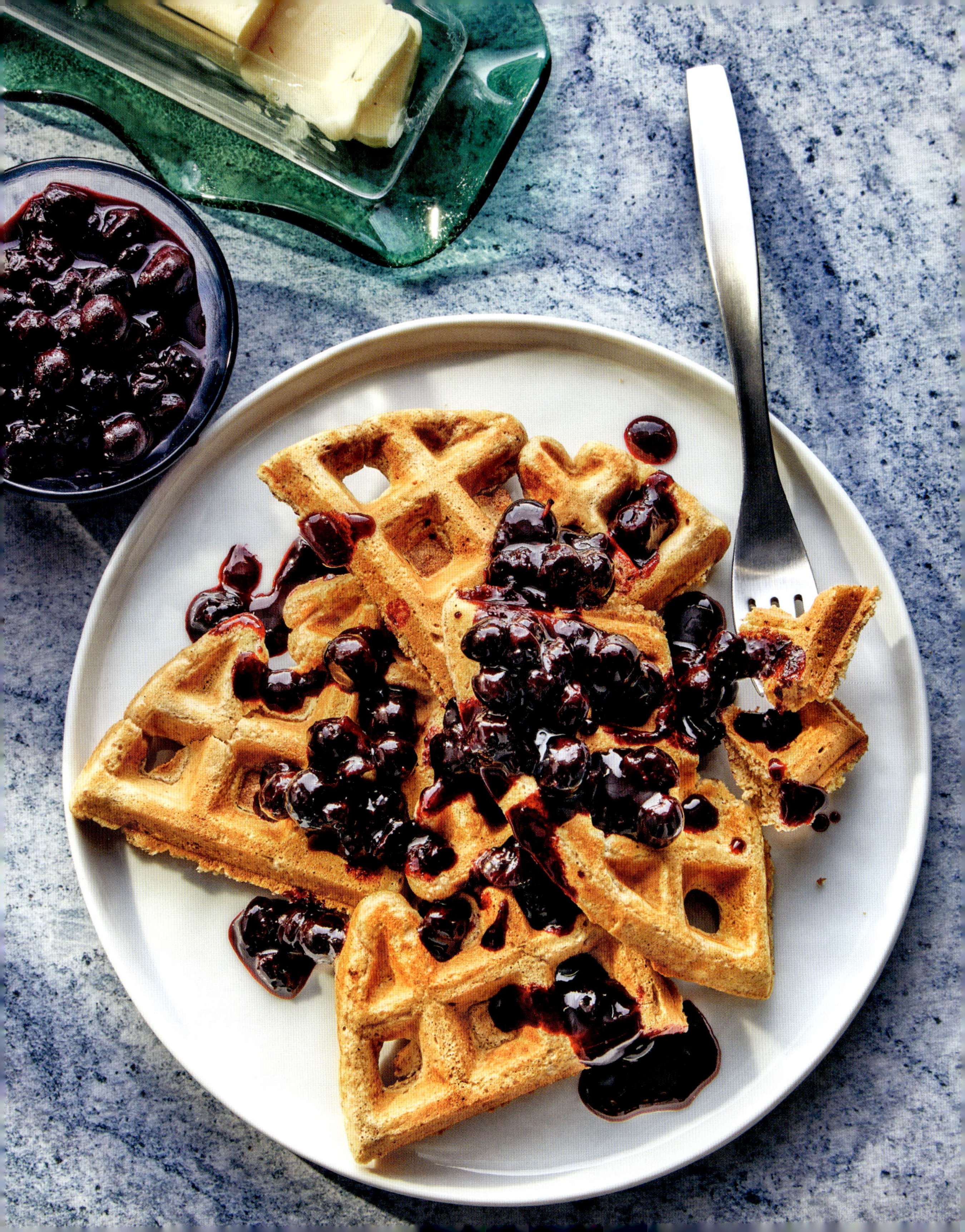

TO MAKE THE COMPOTE

1. In a medium saucepan over medium heat, bring all the ingredients to a simmer and cook, stirring occasionally, until the blueberries break down and the sauce starts to thicken, about 30 minutes. You should have about 2 cups [480 ml] of compote. Cool slightly before using, or cool fully to store. The compote will last in an airtight container in the refrigerator for 1 week.

TO MAKE THE WAFFLES

1. Preheat the oven to 200°F [100°C]. Place a wire rack on a baking sheet in the oven.

2. In a medium bowl, sift together the flour, sugar, salt, baking powder, and baking soda.

3. In a small saucepan over medium-low heat, melt the unsalted butter and cannabutter together, stirring to combine.

4. Using a rubber spatula, scrape the butters into a medium bowl and whisk in the sour cream, milk, and eggs. Add the flour mixture and stir to combine.

5. Heat your waffle iron and spray it with cooking spray. Cook the waffles per the machine's instructions. Place the cooked waffles on the prepared baking sheet in the oven to stay warm, and re-spray the waffle iron between batches.

6. To serve, place 2 waffles on each plate, top with about 6 Tbsp [90 g] of compote, and garnish with lemon zest. The waffles will keep, in an airtight container in the refrigerator, for up to 5 days and in the freezer for up to 2 months. To reheat them, pop them in the toaster.

CANNABIS CORN BREAD WITH HOT HONEY CANNABUTTER

- ✦ MAKES ONE 9 IN [23 CM] PAN (16 SLICES)
- ✦ SERVING SIZE: 1 SLICE PLUS 1½ TSP HOT HONEY CANNABUTTER
- ✦ DOSAGE PER SERVING: FEELIN' GOOD (5 TO 6 MG THC); FOR SKY HIGH (10 TO 12 MG) USE ½ CUP UNSALTED BUTTER AND 1 TBSP CANNABUTTER IN HOT HONEY CANNABUTTER AND 12 TBSP UNSALTED BUTTER AND 1 TBSP CANNABUTTER IN CORN BREAD
- ✦ FOR VIRGIN (0 MG) SKIP CANNABUTTER IN HOT HONEY CANNABUTTER AND CORN BREAD

FOR THE HOT HONEY CANNABUTTER

½ cup [110 g] unsalted butter, at room temperature and cubed

1¼ tsp Cannabutter, at room temperature (page 15)

3 Tbsp honey

2 Tbsp hot sauce

¼ tsp kosher salt

FOR THE CORN BREAD

1½ cups [210 g] stone-ground cornmeal

1 cup [140 g] all-purpose flour

1½ Tbsp baking powder

1½ tsp kosher salt

½ tsp baking soda

12 Tbsp [165 g] unsalted butter

1¼ tsp Cannabutter (page 15)

2¼ cups [540 ml] buttermilk

½ cup [120 ml] molasses

3 large eggs

CONTINUED →

TO MAKE THE HOT HONEY CANNABUTTER

1. Combine all the ingredients in a food processor and pulse until smooth and uniform. The butter will last in an airtight container in the refrigerator for up to 1 week.

TO MAKE THE CORN BREAD

1. Preheat the oven to 375°F [190°C].

2. In a medium bowl, whisk together the cornmeal, flour, baking powder, salt, and baking soda.

3. In a 9 in [23 cm] cast-iron skillet over medium heat, melt the unsalted butter, swirling the pan until it smells nutty and brown flecks form in the bottom of the pan, about 5 minutes.

4. Remove from the heat, coat the sides of the skillet with the butter, then pour the butter into a medium bowl. Add the cannabutter to the bowl and stir until it's melted.

5. Whisk in the buttermilk, molasses, and eggs. Whisk in the flour mixture until a thick batter forms.

6. Pour the batter into the still-hot cast-iron skillet and bake until the top is an amber brown and a cake tester inserted into the center comes out clean, about 35 minutes.

7. Cool in the skillet for 10 minutes, then cut into 16 wedges. Slather 1½ tsp of hot honey cannabutter on each warm wedge of corn bread. The corn bread will last, wrapped tightly with plastic wrap, at room temperature for 3 days, in the refrigerator for 1 week, or in the freezer for 1 month.

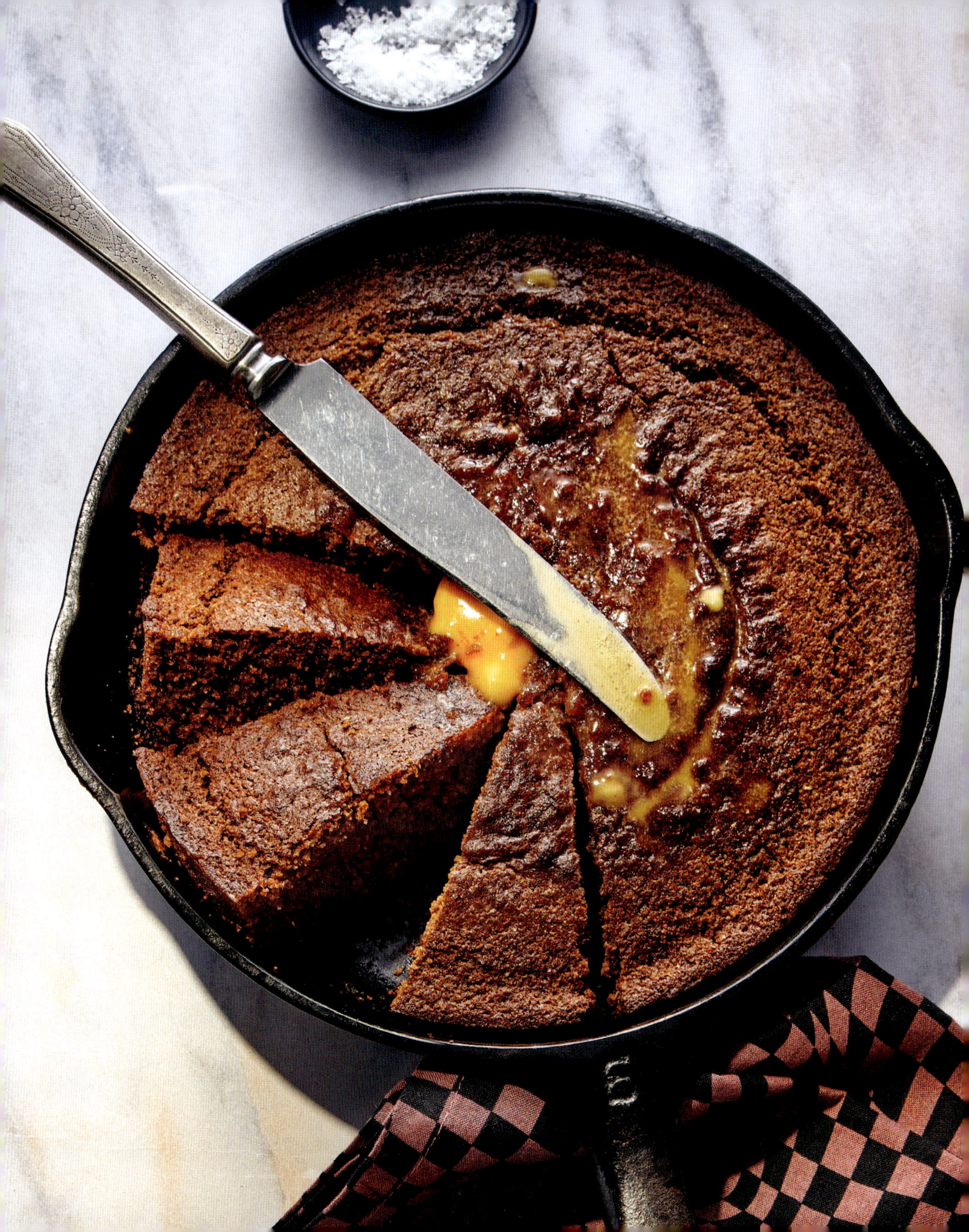

BACON CHEDDAR SCALLION BISCUITS

- **MAKES 12 BISCUITS**
- **SERVING SIZE: 1 BISCUIT**
- **DOSAGE PER SERVING: FEELIN' GOOD (5 TO 6 MG THC); FOR SKY HIGH (10 TO 12 MG) USE 7 TBSP UNSALTED BUTTER AND 4 TSP CANNABUTTER**
- **FOR VIRGIN (0 MG) USE 9 TBSP UNSALTED BUTTER ONLY**

8 oz [230 g] slab bacon, chopped

2 cups [280 g] all-purpose flour

2 tsp baking powder

½ tsp baking soda

½ tsp kosher salt

½ cup [110 g] cold, unsalted butter, cubed

2 tsp cold Cannabutter (page 15), cubed

1 cup [80 g] grated sharp cheddar

1 cup [75 g] sliced scallions

½ cup [120 ml] buttermilk

2 Tbsp melted, unsalted butter, for brushing

1. In a cast-iron skillet over medium heat, cook the bacon until it is partially rendered, about 5 minutes. Drain and set aside.

2. Preheat the oven to 450°F [230°C]. Line a baking sheet with parchment paper or a silicone baking mat.

3. In large bowl, whisk together the flour, baking powder, baking soda, and salt. Add the cold unsalted butter and cannabutter and, with a fork or your fingers, mix them in until the consistency is like wet sand. Fold in the reserved bacon, cheddar, and scallions.

4. Make a well in the center, pour in the buttermilk, and mix just until the dough forms.

5. Drop 2 in [5 cm] wide mounds of dough onto the prepared baking sheet, brush them with the melted butter, and bake until they're golden brown and puffy, 12 to 14 minutes.

6. Eat them hot out of the oven, or cool them on a wire rack. The biscuits will last in an airtight container at room temperature for up to 5 days and in the freezer for up to 1 month.

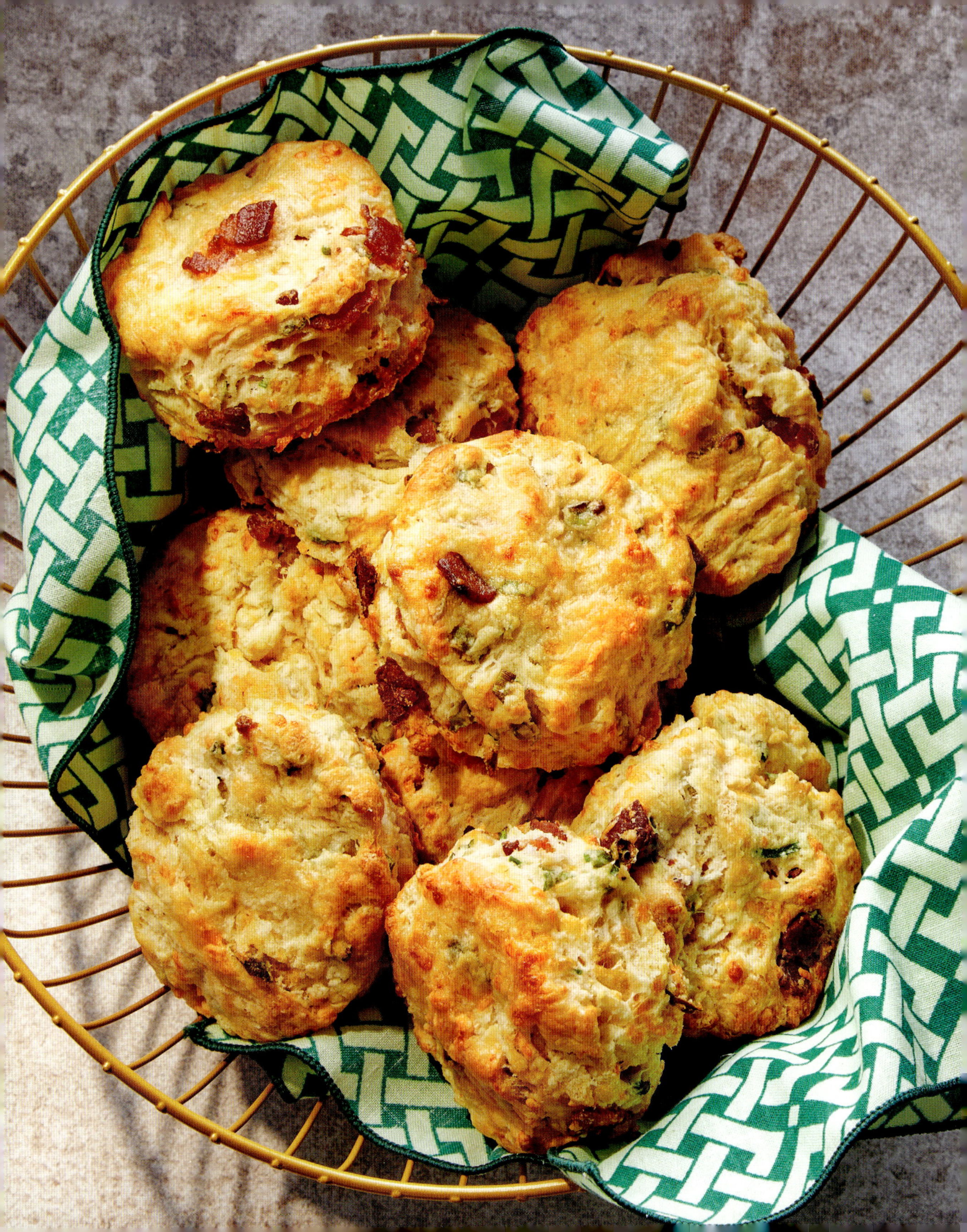

CHAPTER 6

CANDIES, SNACKS, AND SAVOR-IES

Orange You High Yet Gummies [124]

Marijuana Butter Mints [127]

PB & THC Cups [129]

Toasted Coconut Cannabis Truffles [130]

Mixed-Up Nut Toffee [133]

Peanut Butter Raisinet Pretzel Bark [136]

Snoopy Chow [138]

Hot Buttered Pot Corn [141]

Pigs in a Grass Blanket [142]

Herb 'n' Cheese Fatties [145]

Cannabutter Crab Puffs [147]

ORANGE YOU HIGH YET GUMMIES

- **MAKES 150 GUMMIES MADE IN 1 IN [2.5 CM] MOLDS OR 75 GUMMIES MADE IN 2 IN [5 CM] MOLDS**
- **SERVING SIZE: 2 GUMMIES MADE IN 1 IN [2.5 CM] MOLDS OR 1 GUMMY MADE IN 2 IN [5 CM] MOLDS**
- **DOSAGE PER SERVING: FEELIN' GOOD (5 TO 6 MG THC); FOR SKY HIGH (10 TO 12 MG) EAT 4 SMALL GUMMIES OR 2 LARGE GUMMIES**
- **FOR VIRGIN (0 MG) REPLACE CANNABIS GLYCERINE TINCTURE WITH PLAIN FOOD-GRADE GLYCERINE**

¼ cup [60 ml] corn syrup

¼ cup [60 ml] Cannabis Glycerine Tincture (page 15)

1 oz [30 g] unflavored gelatin

3 oz [90 g] orange Jell-O powder

1 Tbsp fresh lemon juice

10 to 12 drops food-grade orange oil

1. Spray gummy molds with cooking spray.

2. In a small saucepan, stir the corn syrup and cannabis glycerine tincture with ½ cup [120 ml] of cold water. Sprinkle in the gelatin, stir, and let bloom for 5 minutes.

3. Add the Jell-O and heat, stirring, over low heat until the gelatin and Jell-O are fully dissolved and the mixture is smooth, 3 to 5 minutes. Remove from the heat and whisk in the lemon juice and orange oil.

4. Pour the mixture into a glass measuring cup and allow the foam to rise to the surface, about 5 minutes. Skim off the foam and, working quickly, use a dropper to fill the prepared molds.

5. Freeze the gummies until set, 20 minutes. Push the gummies out of the molds and set them on a wire rack on the countertop to dry overnight. The gummies will keep in an airtight container in the refrigerator for up to 2 weeks.

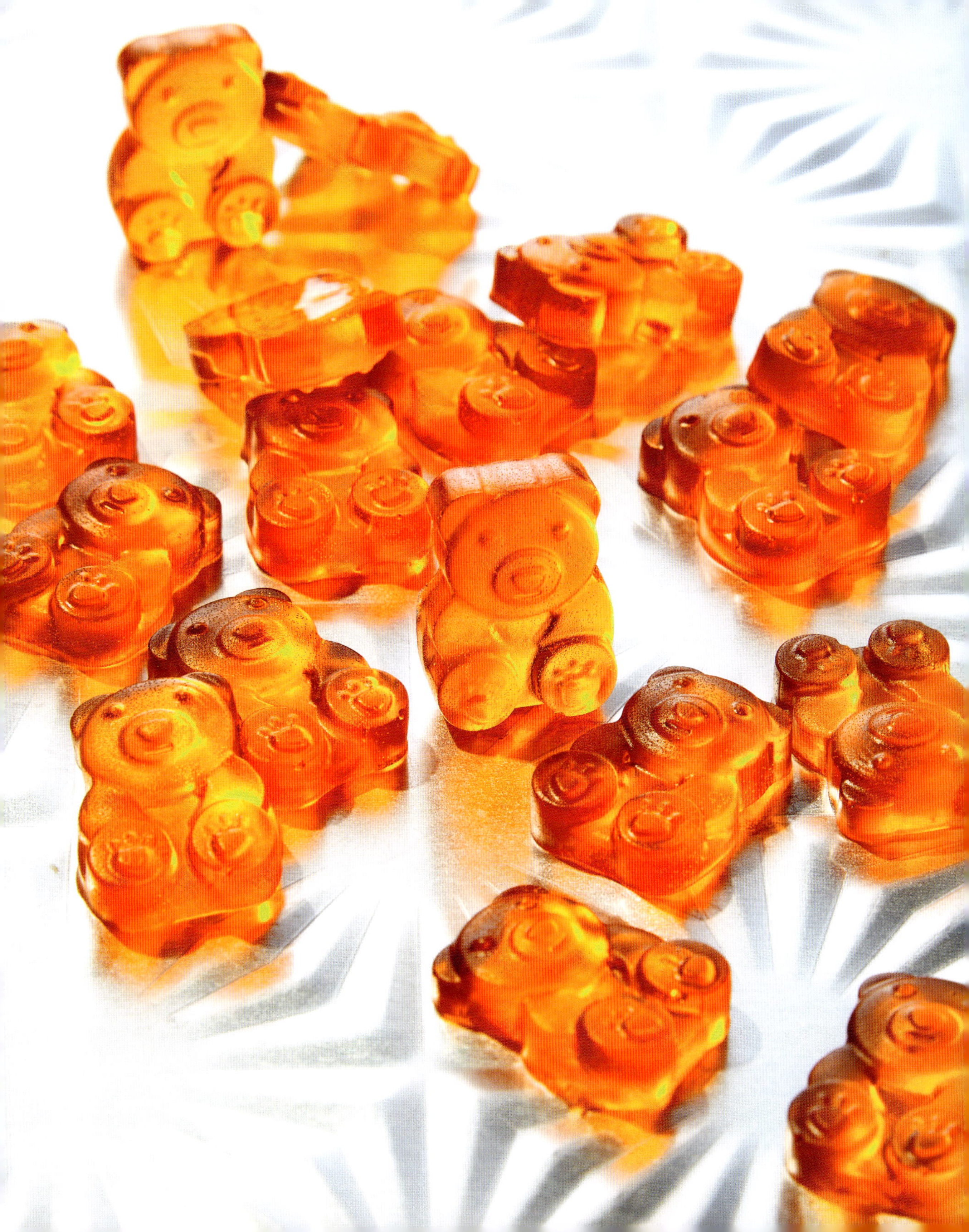

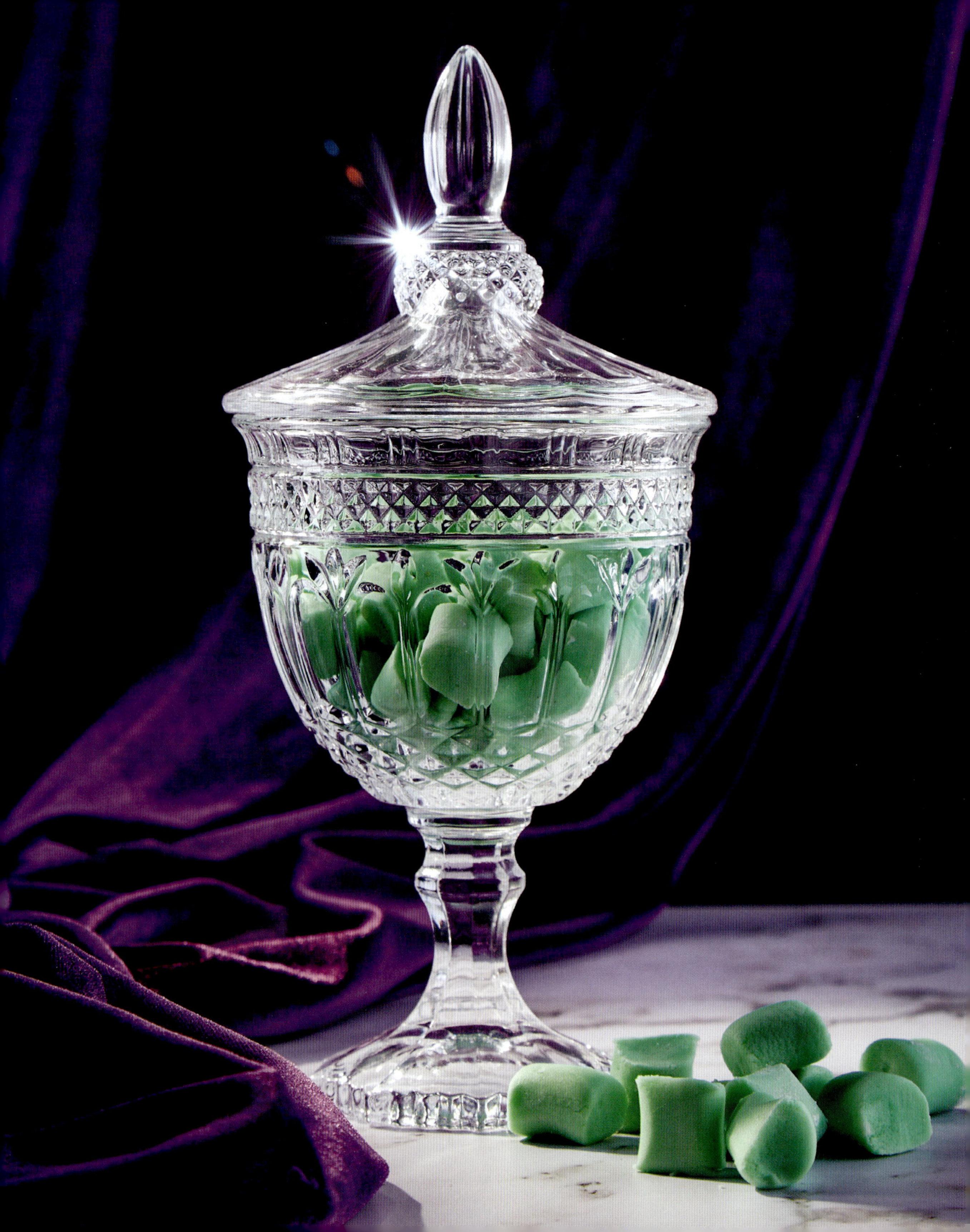

MARIJUANA BUTTER MINTS

- MAKES ABOUT 200 MINTS
- SERVING SIZE: 4 MINTS
- DOSAGE PER SERVING: FEELIN' GOOD (5 TO 6 MG THC); FOR SKY HIGH (10 TO 12 MG) USE 3 TBSP UNSALTED BUTTER AND 5 TBSP CANNABUTTER
- FOR VIRGIN (0 MG) USE 8 TBSP UNSALTED BUTTER ONLY

4 cups [480 g] confectioners' sugar, plus more for dusting

5½ Tbsp [80 g] unsalted butter, at room temperature

2½ Tbsp Cannabutter (page 15), at room temperature

2 Tbsp half-and-half

1 tsp vanilla extract

¼ tsp peppermint extract

Pinch of kosher salt

4 drops green food coloring

1. Set a wire rack over a baking sheet.

2. In the bowl of a stand mixer fitted with the paddle attachment or a food processor, cream all the ingredients together to form a soft, smooth dough.

3. On a surface dusted with confectioners' sugar, form the dough into a ball, press the dough into a disc, and cut it into 6 wedges. Covering the remaining pieces with a damp cloth, roll one piece out into a ½ in [12 mm] rope, and then cut it into ¾ in [2 cm] pieces. Repeat with the remaining dough.

4. Freeze the mints for at least 1 hour and up to 4 hours, or air-dry them on the wire rack overnight. The mints will last in an airtight container in the refrigerator for up to 1 week and in the freezer for several months.

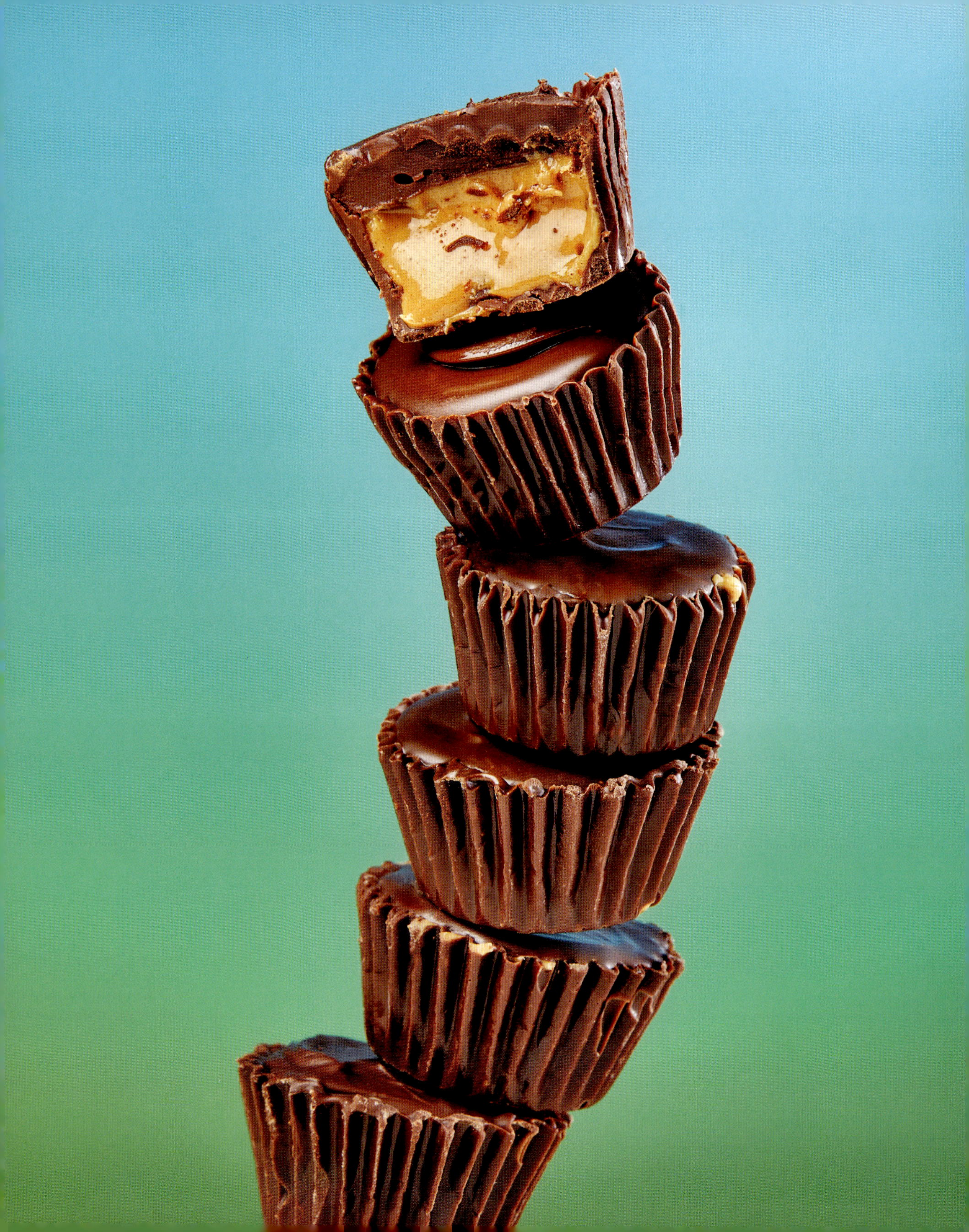

PB & THC CUPS

- **MAKES 12 CANDIES**
- **SERVING SIZE: 1 CANDY**
- **DOSAGE PER SERVING: FEELIN' GOOD (5 TO 6 MG THC); FOR SKY HIGH (10 TO 12 MG) USE 4 TSP CANNABIS COCONUT OIL**
- **FOR VIRGIN (0 MG) SKIP CANNABIS COCONUT OIL**

1 lb [455 g] chocolate chips

2 tsp Cannabis Coconut Oil (page 15)

½ cup [130 g] peanut butter

¼ cup [30 g] confectioners' sugar

½ tsp vanilla extract

¼ tsp kosher salt

1. Line 12 mini muffin cups with muffin liners. In a medium, heavy-walled saucepan over medium-low heat, melt the chocolate chips and cannabis coconut oil together, stirring occasionally, until smooth.

2. Pour 1 tsp of the melted chocolate mixture into each liner, filling the bottom. Chill the tin in the freezer to set the chocolate, 10 minutes.

3. In a food processor, pulse the peanut butter, confectioners' sugar, vanilla, and salt until smooth and uniform. Mound 2 tsp of the peanut butter mixture into each liner, leaving room between the liner and the peanut butter to pour more chocolate.

4. Divide the remaining chocolate evenly among the liners, covering the peanut butter mixture completely. Chill the cups in the freezer to set the chocolate, another 10 minutes. The peanut butter cups will last in an airtight container in the refrigerator for up to 5 days or in the freezer for up to 1 month.

CANDIES, SNACKS, AND SAVORIES

TOASTED COCONUT CANNABIS TRUFFLES

- **MAKES 24 TRUFFLES**
- **SERVING SIZE: 1 TRUFFLE**
- **DOSAGE PER SERVING: FEELIN' GOOD (5 TO 6 MG THC); FOR SKY HIGH (10 TO 12 MG) USE 8 TSP CANNABIS COCONUT OIL**
- **FOR VIRGIN (0 MG) SKIP CANNABIS COCONUT OIL**

5½ cups [440 g] unsweetened shredded coconut

One 14 oz [420 ml] can sweetened condensed milk

4 tsp Cannabis Coconut Oil (page 15)

2 Tbsp confectioners' sugar

3 cups [540 g] semisweet chocolate chips

½ tsp kosher salt

CONTINUED →

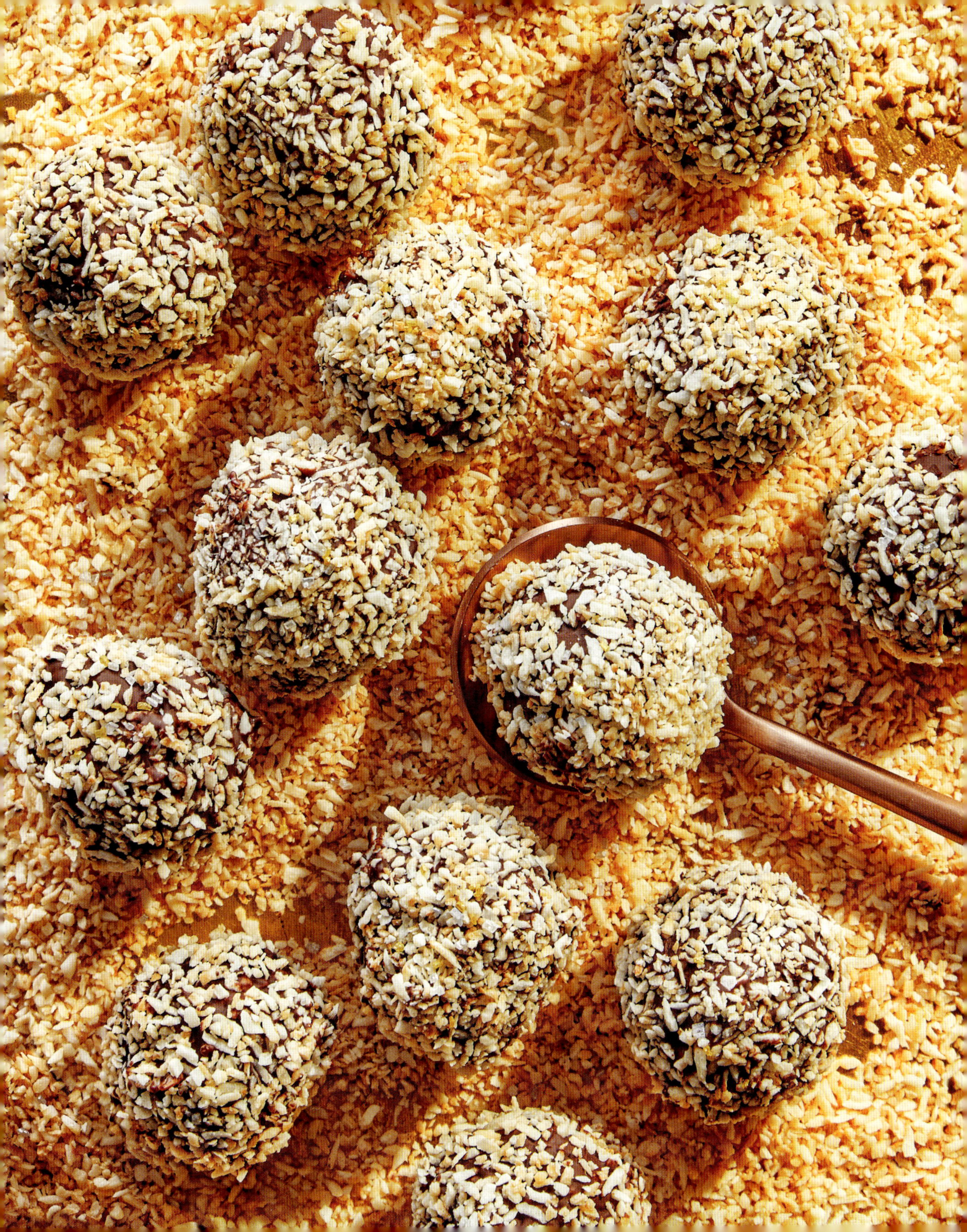

1. Preheat the oven to 325°F [165°C]. Line two baking sheets with parchment paper or silicone baking mats.

2. In a medium bowl, mix together 3 cups [240 g] of the shredded coconut, the sweetened condensed milk, and the cannabis coconut oil. With wet hands, roll the mixture, 1 Tbsp at a time, into 24 balls and place them on one of the prepared baking sheets. Chill for 1 hour.

3. Spread the remaining 2½ cups [200 g] of shredded coconut evenly on the other prepared baking sheet and toast it until golden brown, about 5 minutes. Cool to room temperature, transfer to a small bowl, sift in the confectioners' sugar, and mix until fully combined.

4. In a heavy-walled, medium saucepan over medium-low heat, melt the chocolate chips and salt together, stirring, until smooth, 3 to 4 minutes. Working one at a time, use a fork or toothpick to dip the truffles in the chocolate, tilting to coat fully.

5. Roll each truffle in the toasted coconut and return it to the baking sheet. Chill to set the chocolate, 30 minutes more. The truffles will last in an airtight container in the refrigerator for up to 1 week.

MIXED-UP NUT TOFFEE

- **MAKES 24 SERVINGS**
- **SERVING SIZE: ONE 2½ OZ [70 G] CHUNK**
- **DOSAGE PER SERVING: FEELIN' GOOD (5 TO 6 MG THC); FOR SKY HIGH (10 TO 12 MG) USE 1¾ CUPS PLUS 1 TBSP UNSALTED BUTTER AND 8 TSP CANNABUTTER**
- **FOR VIRGIN (0 MG) 2 CUPS PLUS 4 TSP UNSALTED BUTTER**

2 cups [280 g] chopped, roasted mixed nuts

2 cups [400 g] granulated sugar

2 cups [440 g] unsalted butter

4 tsp Cannabutter (page 15)

1 tsp kosher salt

3 cups [540 g] milk chocolate chips

1. Line a baking sheet with parchment paper or a silicone baking mat and spread the nuts evenly on it.

2. In a medium Dutch oven over medium-low heat, melt the sugar, unsalted butter, cannabutter, and salt together, stirring occasionally, until the sugar is dissolved, 10 to 12 minutes. Attach a candy thermometer to the side of the Dutch oven.

3. Increase the heat to medium and bring the mixture to a boil. Stirring slowly and occasionally, cook the toffee until it's a deep amber color and the thermometer reads 285°F [140°C], about 15 minutes.

4. Pour the toffee over the nuts, spreading it evenly with a spatula. Sprinkle the chocolate chips evenly over the top and spread them evenly over the toffee as they melt.

5. Chill the toffee until set, about 1 hour. Cut into 24 equal pieces as evenly as possible. The toffee will keep in an airtight container in the refrigerator for up to 1 week or in the freezer for up to 1 month.

MIXED-UP
NUT TOFFEE

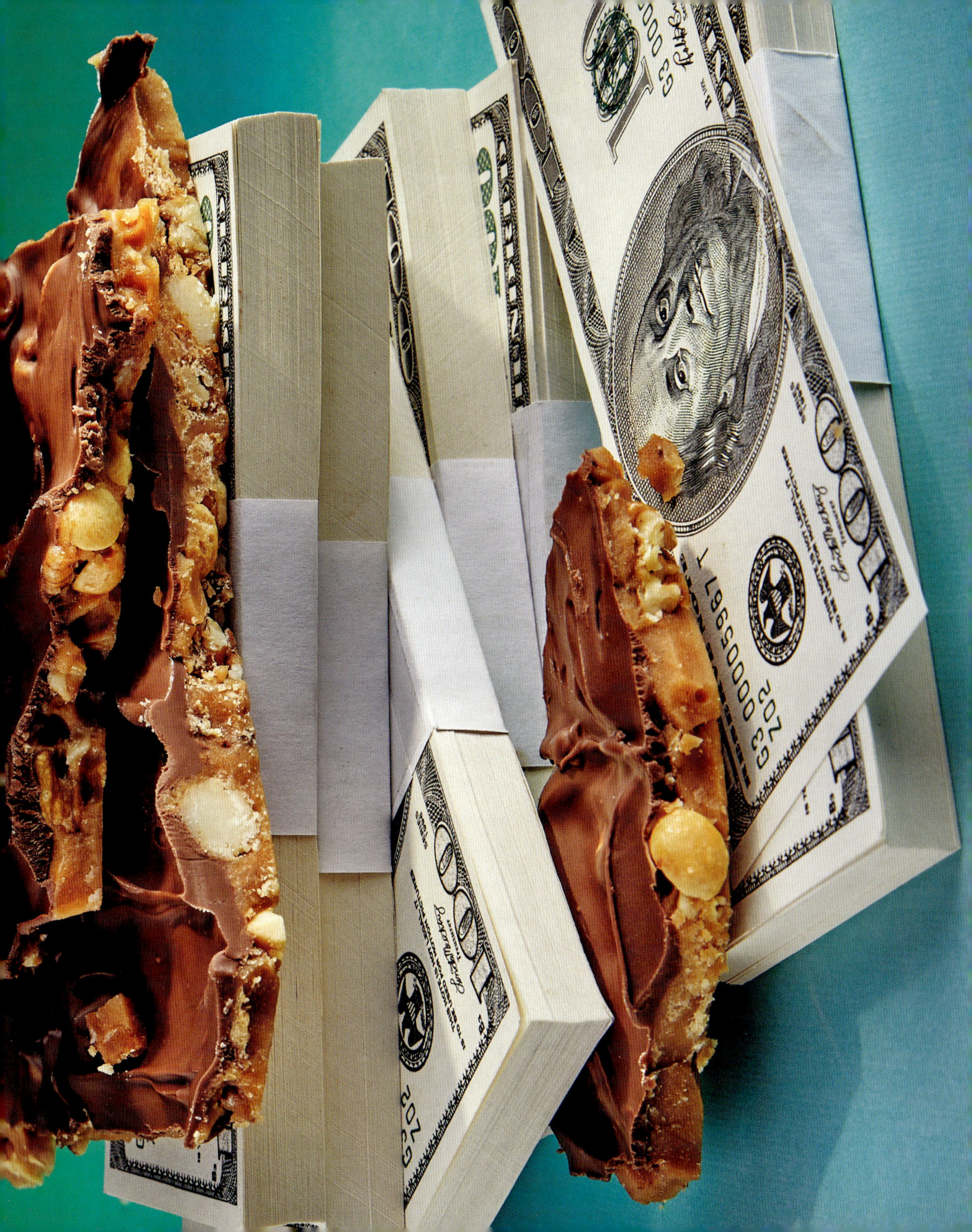

PEANUT BUTTER RAISINET PRETZEL BARK

- **MAKES 20 SERVINGS**
- **SERVING SIZE: ONE 1 OZ [30 G] CHUNK**
- **DOSAGE PER SERVING: FEELIN' GOOD (5 TO 6 MG THC); FOR SKY HIGH (10 TO 12 MG) USE 3 TBSP PEANUT BUTTER AND 2 TBSP CANNABUTTER**
- **FOR VIRGIN (0 MG) USE 5 TBSP PEANUT BUTTER ONLY**

1¾ cups [315 g] white chocolate chips

¼ cup [65 g] creamy peanut butter

1 Tbsp Cannabutter (page 15)

¾ cup [30 g] roughly crushed thin pretzels

½ cup [100 g] Raisinets

1. Line a baking sheet with parchment paper or a silicone baking mat. In a heavy-walled, medium saucepan over low heat, melt the white chocolate chips, peanut butter, and cannabutter together, stirring often, until smooth, about 5 minutes.

2. Remove the pan from the heat, stir in the pretzels and Raisinets, and immediately pour the mixture onto the prepared baking sheet. Using a rubber spatula, spread it out evenly in a thin layer. Score the top of the bark with a knife into 20 equal portions.

3. Chill until set, about 45 minutes. Cut along the scored lines. The bark will keep in an airtight container in the refrigerator for up to 1 week or in the freezer for up to 1 month.

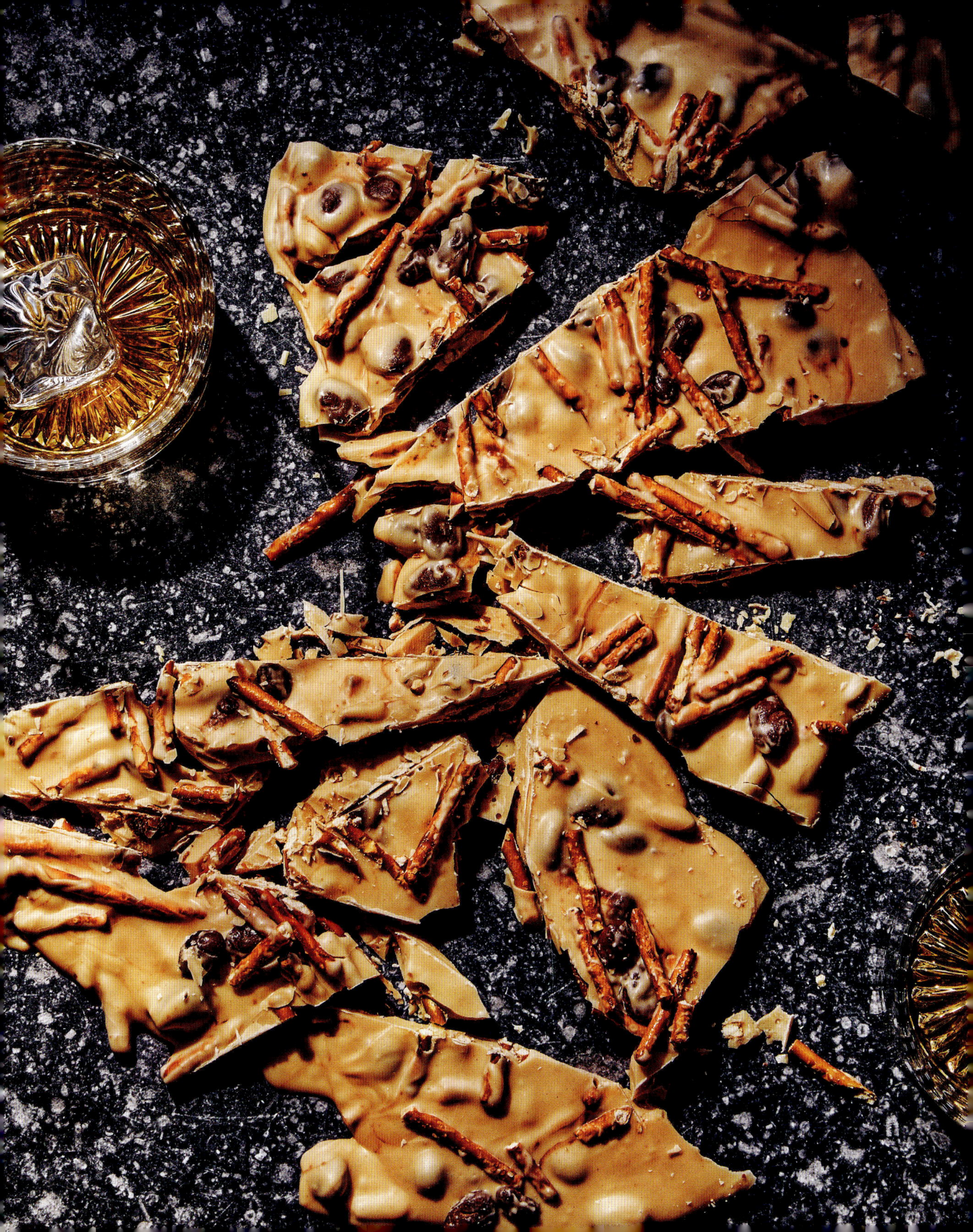

SNOOPY CHOW

- **MAKES ABOUT 10 CUPS [1040 G]**
- **SERVING SIZE: ½ CUP [50 G]**
- **DOSAGE PER SERVING: FEELIN' GOOD (5 TO 6 MG THC); FOR SKY HIGH (10 TO 12 MG) USE 2 TBSP UNSALTED BUTTER AND 2 TBSP CANNABUTTER**
- **FOR VIRGIN (0 MG) USE 4 TBSP UNSALTED BUTTER ONLY**

12 oz [340 g] Rice Chex, or another Chex of your choice

1 cup [180 g] semisweet chocolate chips

½ cup [130 g] creamy peanut butter

3 Tbsp unsalted butter

1 Tbsp Cannabutter (page 15)

1 tsp vanilla extract

1½ cups [180 g] confectioners' sugar

1. Place the Chex in a large bowl.

2. In a heavy-bottomed, medium saucepan over medium-low heat, melt the chocolate chips, peanut butter, unsalted butter, and cannabutter together, stirring, until smooth and uniform, about 5 minutes.

3. Remove from the heat, stir in the vanilla, and pour the mixture over the Chex. Stir to coat evenly.

4. Sift the confectioners' sugar over the top and stir to coat evenly. The chow will keep in an airtight container in the refrigerator for up to 1 week.

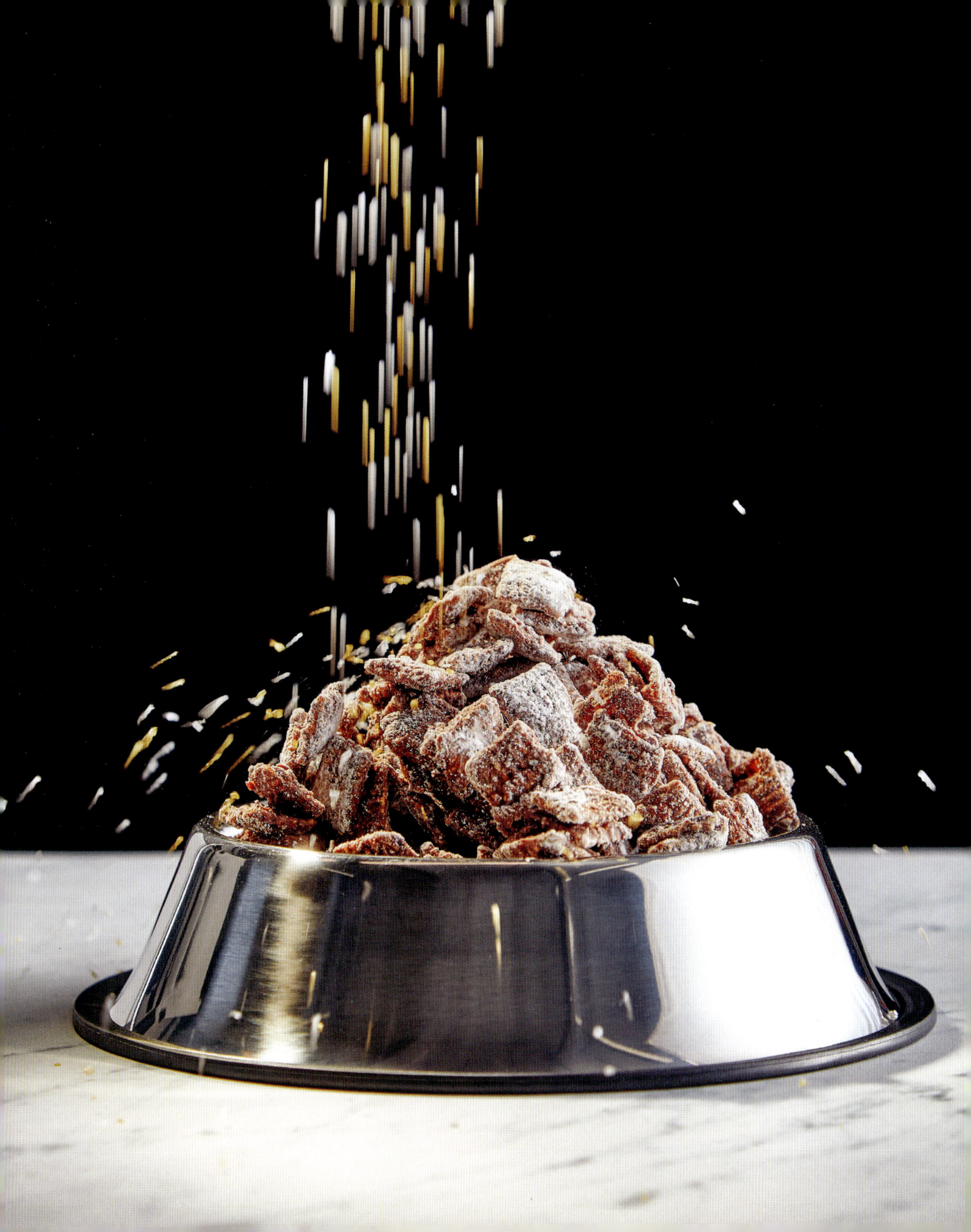

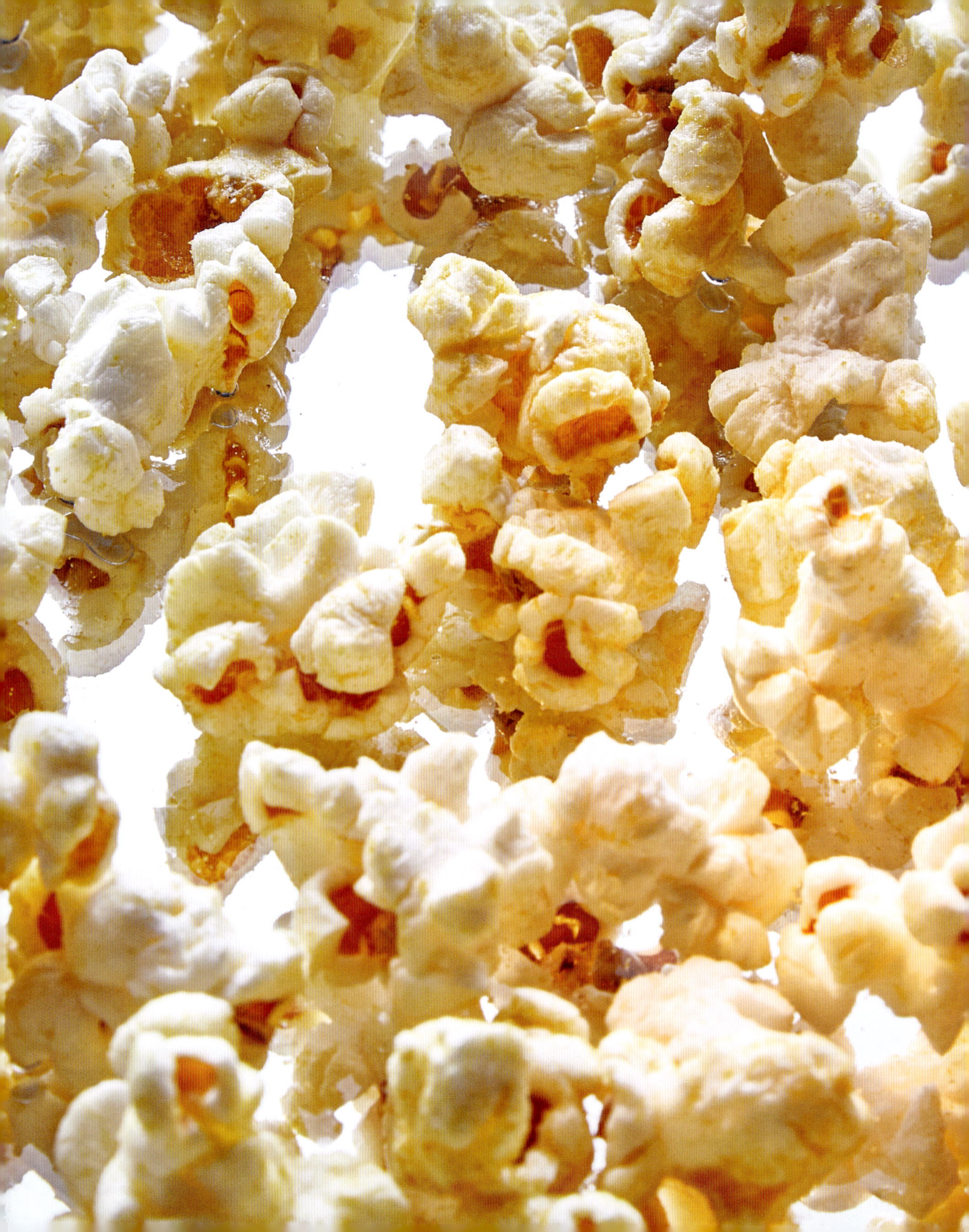

HOT BUTTERED POT CORN

- **MAKES 18 CUPS [240 G]**
- **SERVING SIZE: 3 CUPS [40 G]**
- **DOSAGE PER SERVING: FEELIN' GOOD (5 TO 6 MG THC); FOR SKY HIGH (10 TO 12 MG) USE 2 TSP CANNABUTTER**
- **FOR VIRGIN (0 MG) SKIP CANNABUTTER**

3 Tbsp vegetable oil

¾ cup [150 g] popcorn kernels

½ cup [110] unsalted butter

1 tsp Cannabutter (page 15)

¾ tsp fine sea salt

1. In a Dutch oven over medium heat, heat the vegetable oil until shimmering. Add the popcorn, cover, and cook the popcorn, shaking the Dutch oven every few seconds. It will start popping in 3 to 5 minutes. Continue shaking and cooking until there are 3 seconds between pops, about 5 minutes more.

2. In a small saucepan over medium-low heat, melt the unsalted butter and cannabutter together, swirling to combine. Transfer the popcorn to a big mixing bowl, drizzle the melted butter on the popcorn, and sprinkle on the salt. Invert another bowl of the same size over the bowl of popcorn, and, holding the bowls together at the seams, shake them well to fully coat the popcorn.

PIGS IN A GRASS BLANKET

- MAKES 24 PIGS IN A BLANKET
- SERVING SIZE: 2 PIGS IN A BLANKET
- DOSAGE PER SERVING: FEELIN' GOOD (5 TO 6 MG THC); FOR SKY HIGH (10 TO 12 MG) USE 1 TBSP UNSALTED BUTTER AND 4 TSP CANNABUTTER
- FOR VIRGIN (0 MG) USE 3 TBSP UNSALTED BUTTER

One 8 oz [230 g] tube crescent roll dough in a sheet

2 Tbsp unsalted butter

2 tsp Cannabutter (page 15)

24 mini hot dogs, or 8 regular hot dogs sliced into thirds

Everything seasoning or flaky sea salt, for garnish

Mustard, for serving

1. Preheat the oven to 350°F [180°C]. Line a baking sheet with parchment paper or a silicone baking mat.

2. Unroll the crescent roll sheet and separate it on the perforated lines into triangles. Cut each triangle vertically into three thinner triangles, for a total of 24 triangles.

3. In a small saucepan over medium-low heat, melt the unsalted butter and cannabutter together, swirling to combine. Using a pastry brush, brush each triangle with melted butter.

4. Place one mini dog across the bottom of a triangle and roll it up in the dough. Place it on the prepared baking sheet seam-side down. Repeat with the remaining dough and dogs.

5. Brush the top of each pig in a blanket with the remaining butter. Sprinkle everything seasoning over the top. Bake until golden brown and puffy, about 20 minutes. Serve immediately with mustard on the side.

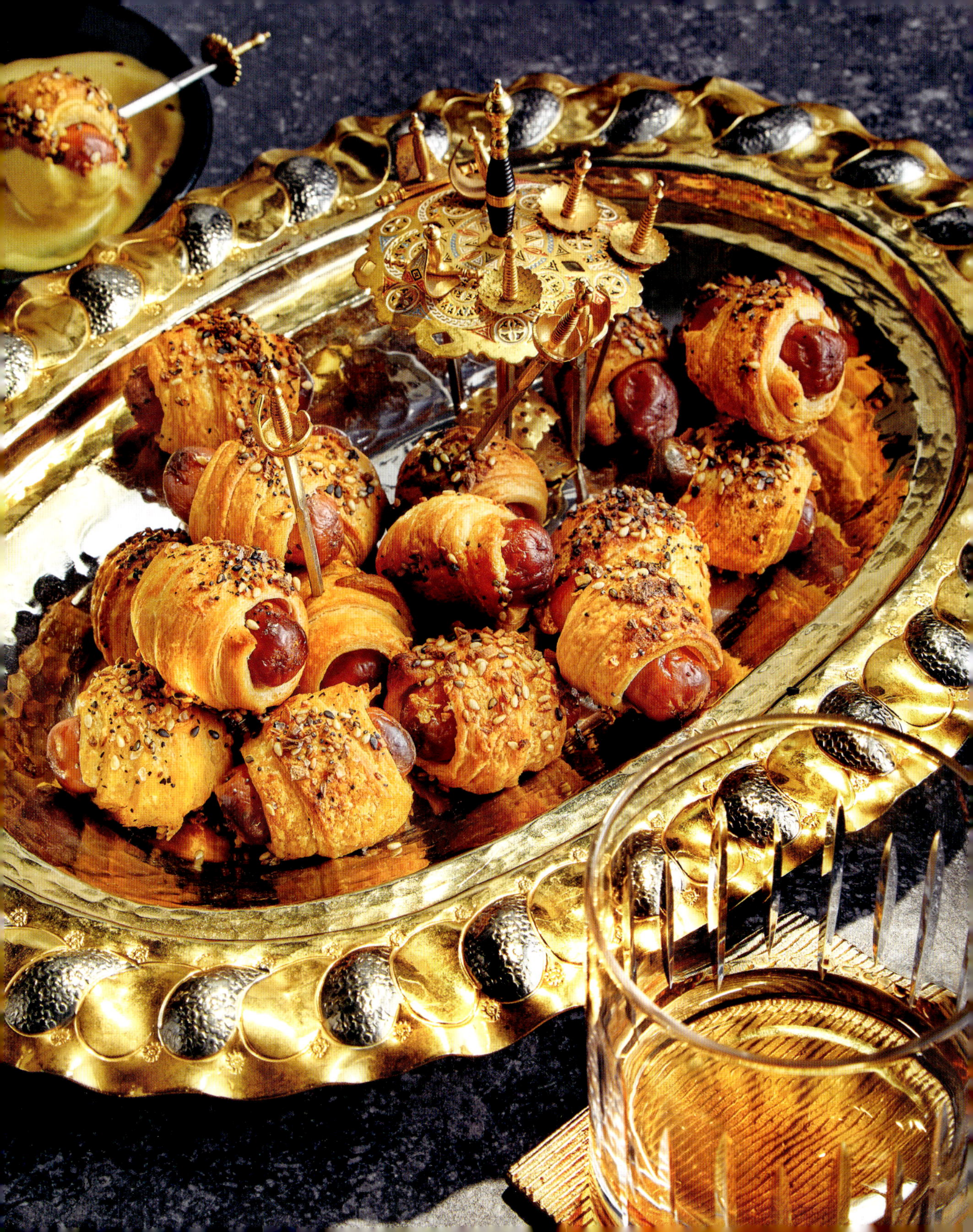

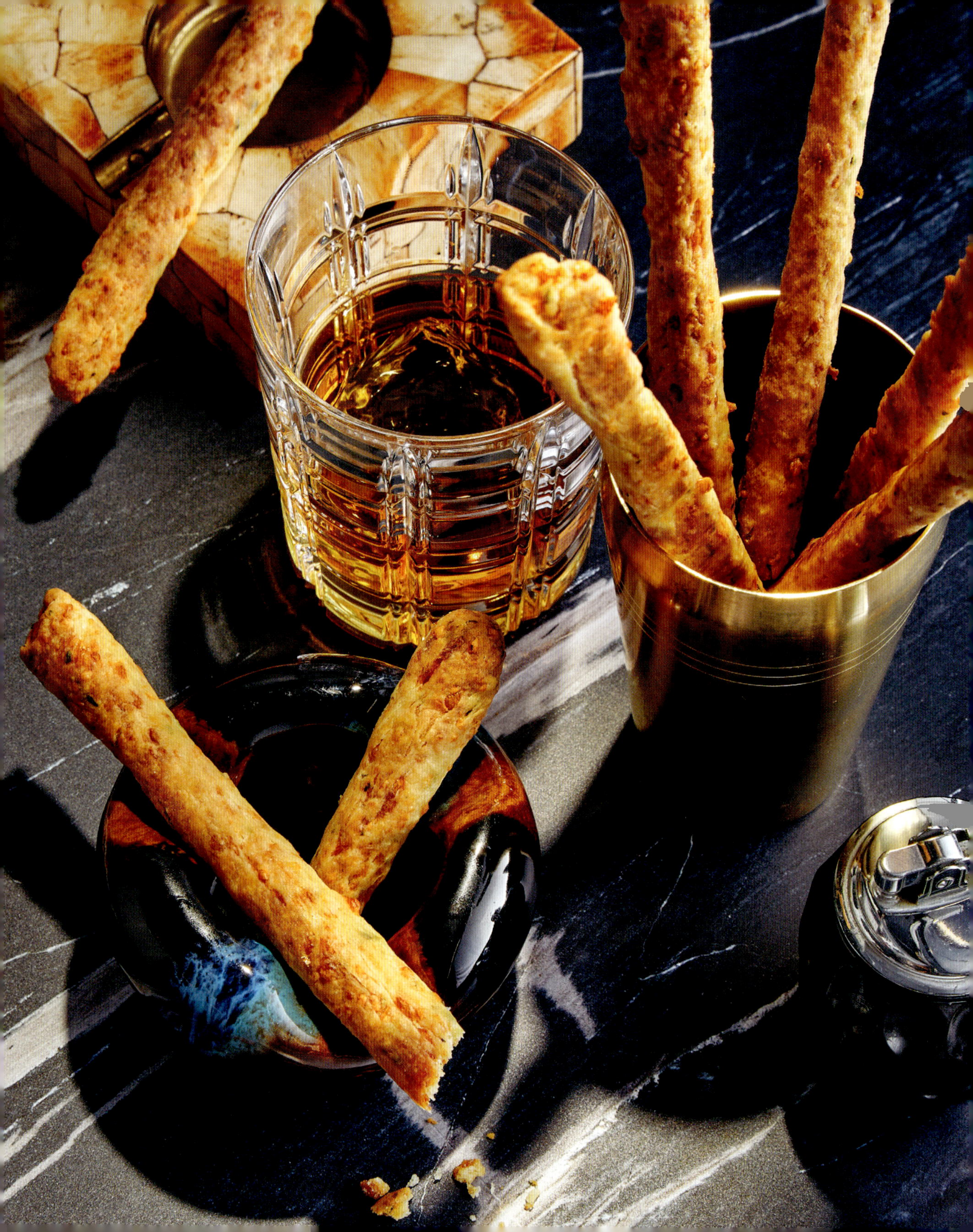

HERB 'N' CHEESE FATTIES

- ◆ **MAKES 24 CHEESE STRAWS**
- ◆ **SERVING SIZE: 1 CHEESE STRAW**
- ◆ **DOSAGE PER SERVING: FEELIN' GOOD (5 TO 6 MG THC); FOR SKY HIGH (10 TO 12 MG) USE 7 TBSP UNSALTED BUTTER AND 2½ TBSP CANNABUTTER**
- ◆ **FOR VIRGIN (0 MG) USE 9 TBSP UNSALTED BUTTER ONLY**

1⅔ cups [230 g] all-purpose flour, plus more for dusting

1¼ tsp dry mustard

1 tsp kosher salt

½ tsp garlic powder (optional)

8 oz [230 g] Gruyère cheese, grated

½ cup [110 g] unsalted butter, at room temperature

4 tsp Cannabutter (page 15), at room temperature

1 Tbsp minced thyme

¼ cup [60 ml] heavy cream

CONTINUED →

CANDIES, SNACKS, AND SAVORIES

1. Preheat the oven to 425°F [220°C]. Line a baking sheet with parchment paper or a silicone baking mat.

2. In a medium bowl, whisk together the flour, mustard, salt, and garlic powder, if using. In a food processor, pulse the cheese, unsalted butter, cannabutter, and thyme until smooth. Fold in the flour mixture. Add the cream and pulse to form a thick dough.

3. Turn the dough out onto a lightly floured surface and knead for 5 minutes. Working with 2 Tbsp at a time, roll the dough into 9 by ½ in [23 cm by 13 mm] ropes. Transfer them to the prepared baking sheet, spacing them ½ in [12 mm] apart.

4. Bake until crisp and golden brown, 12 to 14 minutes. Cool for 10 minutes before serving.

5. Repeat with or freeze the remaining dough. It will keep, in an airtight container, in the freezer for up to 1 month. Baked fatties will last, in an airtight container at room temperature, for up to 5 days.

CANNABUTTER CRAB PUFFS

- ◆ MAKES 24 CRAB PUFFS
- ◆ SERVING SIZE: 2 CRAB PUFFS
- ◆ DOSAGE PER SERVING: FEELIN' GOOD (5 TO 6 MG THC); FOR SKY HIGH (10 TO 12 MG) USE 2 TBSP UNSALTED BUTTER AND 4 TSP CANNABUTTER
- ◆ FOR VIRGIN (0 MG) SKIP CANNABIS COCONUT OIL

1 package (two 9 by 9 in [23 by 23 cm] sheets) puff pastry, defrosted

1 lb [455 g] lump crabmeat

4 oz [115 g] cream cheese, at room temperature

¼ cup [60 g] mayonnaise

3 Tbsp unsalted butter, at room temperature

2 tsp Cannabutter (page 15), at room temperature

¼ cup [30 g] sliced scallion

3 cloves garlic, minced

1 Tbsp chopped tarragon

1 Tbsp chopped parsley

2 tsp Tabasco

2 tsp Dijon mustard

2 tsp lemon juice

Zest of 1 lemon

1 tsp chopped capers

¼ tsp kosher salt

¼ tsp freshly ground black pepper

¼ tsp paprika

CONTINUED →

CANDIES, SNACKS, AND SAVORIES

1. Preheat the oven to 400°F [200°C]. Spray 24 mini muffin cups with cooking spray. Cut each puff pastry sheet into 12 equal rectangles. Tuck the rectangles into the muffin cups so that they form cups for the crab mixture.

2. In a medium bowl, mix the crabmeat, cream cheese, mayonnaise, unsalted butter, cannabutter, scallion, garlic, tarragon, parsley, Tabasco, mustard, lemon juice, lemon zest, capers, salt, pepper, and paprika until well combined and smooth.

3. Place 1 heaping Tbsp of the crab mixture into each puff pastry cup and bake until the pastry is puffed and golden brown, 20 to 25 minutes. Cool for 5 minutes in the tin before transferring to a serving platter. The crab puffs will last, in an airtight container, in the refrigerator for up to 3 days and in the freezer for up to 1 month.

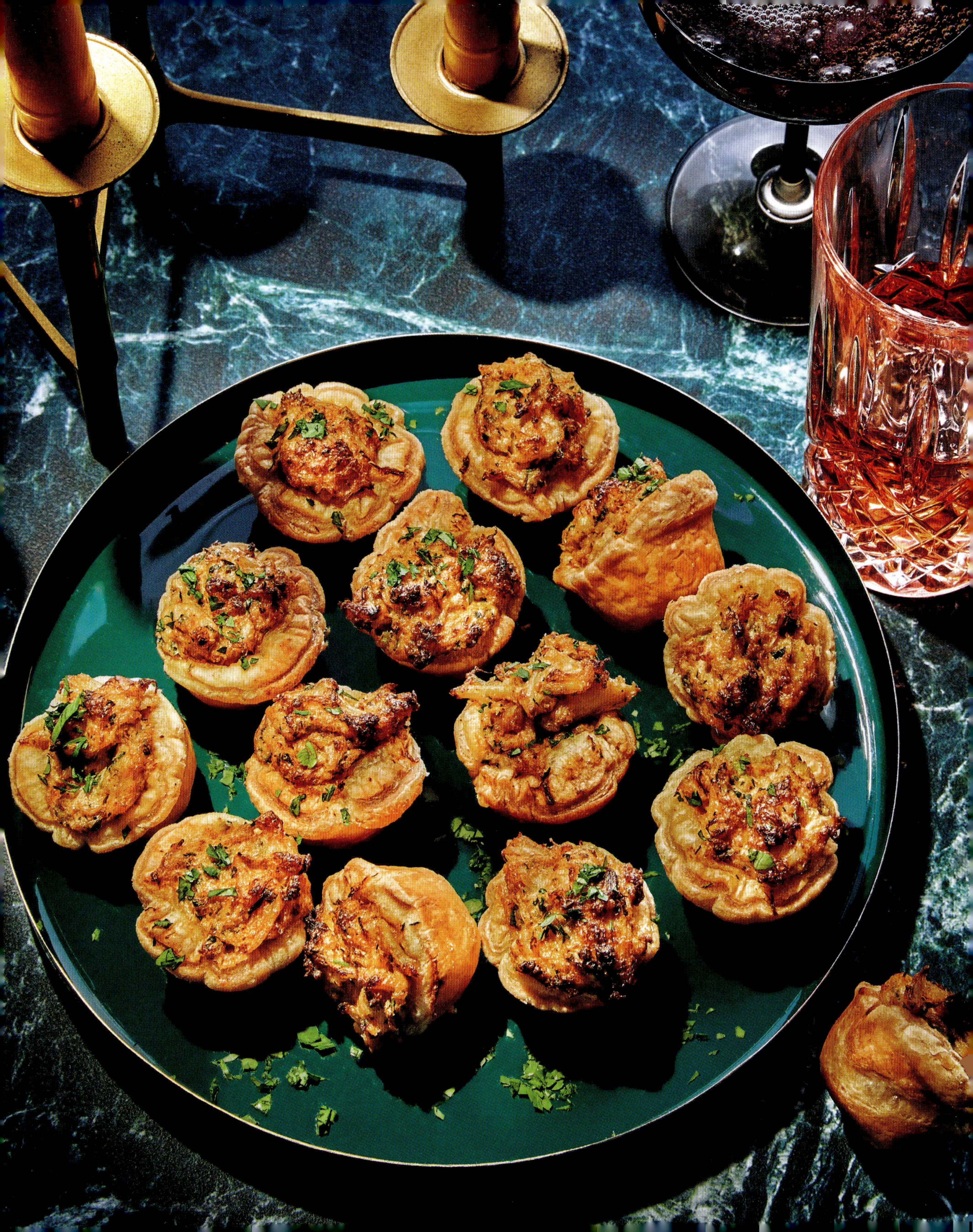

CHAPTER 7

DRINKS

Arnold Palmer in the Weeds [152]

Tha Grass Smoovie [156]

Stoner-berry Shakes [159]

Pot Cocoa [161]

Hot Cannabuttered Rum [162]

Blitz Spritz [166]

Jacked-Up Gin 'n' Juice [169]

ARNOLD PALMER IN THE WEEDS

- ◆ **MAKES 8 SERVINGS**
- ◆ **SERVING SIZE: ABOUT 1 CUP [240 ML]**
- ◆ **DOSAGE PER SERVING: FEELIN' GOOD (5 TO 6 MG THC); FOR SKY HIGH (10 TO 12 MG) USE 1 TSP CANNABIS GLYCERINE TINCTURE IN TEA AND LEMONADE**
- ◆ **FOR VIRGIN (0 MG) SKIP CANNABIS GLYCERINE TINCTURE**

FOR THE SWEET TEA

4 black tea bags

½ cup [100 g] granulated sugar

½ tsp Cannabis Glycerine Tincture (page 15)

FOR THE LEMONADE

½ cup [100 g] granulated sugar

½ tsp Cannabis Glycerine Tincture (page 15)

1 cup [240 ml] fresh lemon juice, from 3 to 5 lemons

FOR THE GARNISH

Lemon slices

Mint sprigs

TO MAKE THE SWEET TEA

1. In a medium saucepan, bring 2 cups [480 ml] of water to a boil. Remove from the heat, add the tea bags, and let steep for 10 minutes.

2. In a pitcher, add the sugar, tincture, and 2 cups [480 ml] of water and stir to combine.

3. Discard the tea bags and pour the hot tea over the sugar water. Stir to dissolve the sugar fully. Chill for 30 minutes, and if you like, serve over ice, garnished with lemon slices and mint sprigs. Makes 4 cups [960 ml].

TO MAKE THE LEMONADE

1. In a small saucepan over medium-low heat, dissolve the sugar in 1 cup [240 ml] of water. Remove from the heat and stir in the tincture.

2. Combine the simple syrup and lemon juice in a pitcher, add 2 cups [480 ml] of cold water, and stir to combine. Chill for 30 minutes, and if you like, serve over ice, garnished with lemon slices. Makes 4 cups [960 ml].

TO MAKE THE ARNOLD PALMER

1. Fill a glass with ice, pour ¾ cup [180 ml] of lemonade over the top, and top with ¾ cup [180 ml] of iced tea. Garnish with lemon slices and mint sprigs.

ARNOLD PALMER
IN THE WEEDS

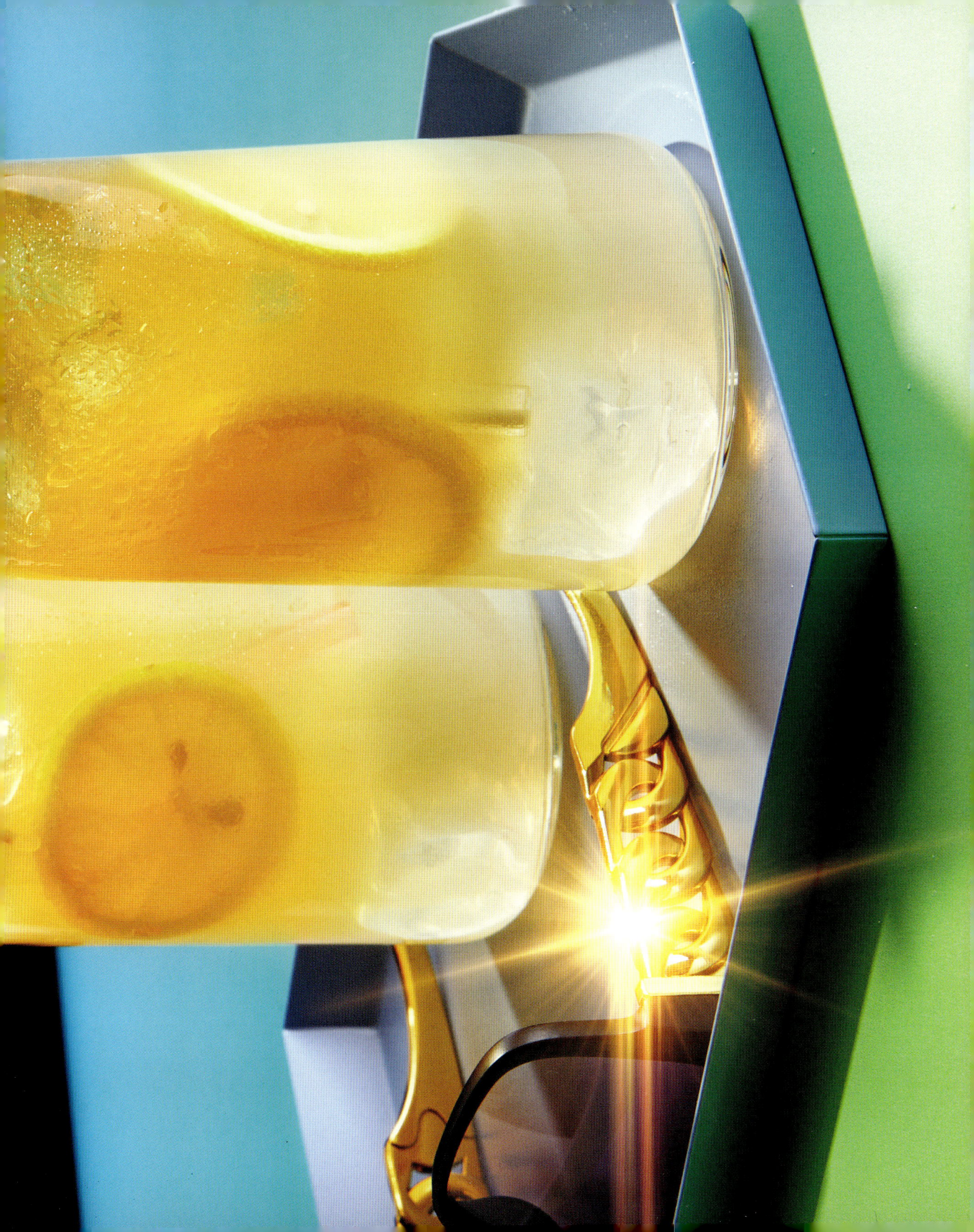

THA GRASS SMOOVIE

- ◆ MAKES ONE 3 CUP [720 ML] SMOOTHIE
- ◆ SERVING SIZE: 1 SMOOTHIE
- ◆ DOSAGE PER SERVING: FEELIN' GOOD (5 TO 6 MG THC); FOR SKY HIGH (10 TO 12 MG) USE ¼ TSP CANNABIS GRAIN-ALCOHOL TINCTURE
- ◆ FOR VIRGIN (0 MG) SKIP CANNABIS GRAIN-ALCOHOL TINCTURE

2 cups [40 g] fresh spinach

1 orange, peeled and quartered

1 banana, sliced

2 cups [480 ml] coconut water

2 Tbsp protein powder (optional)

⅛ tsp or 12 drops Cannabis Grain-Alcohol Tincture (page 18)

In a blender, combine all the ingredients. Blend on high speed until smooth and creamy. Serve immediately.

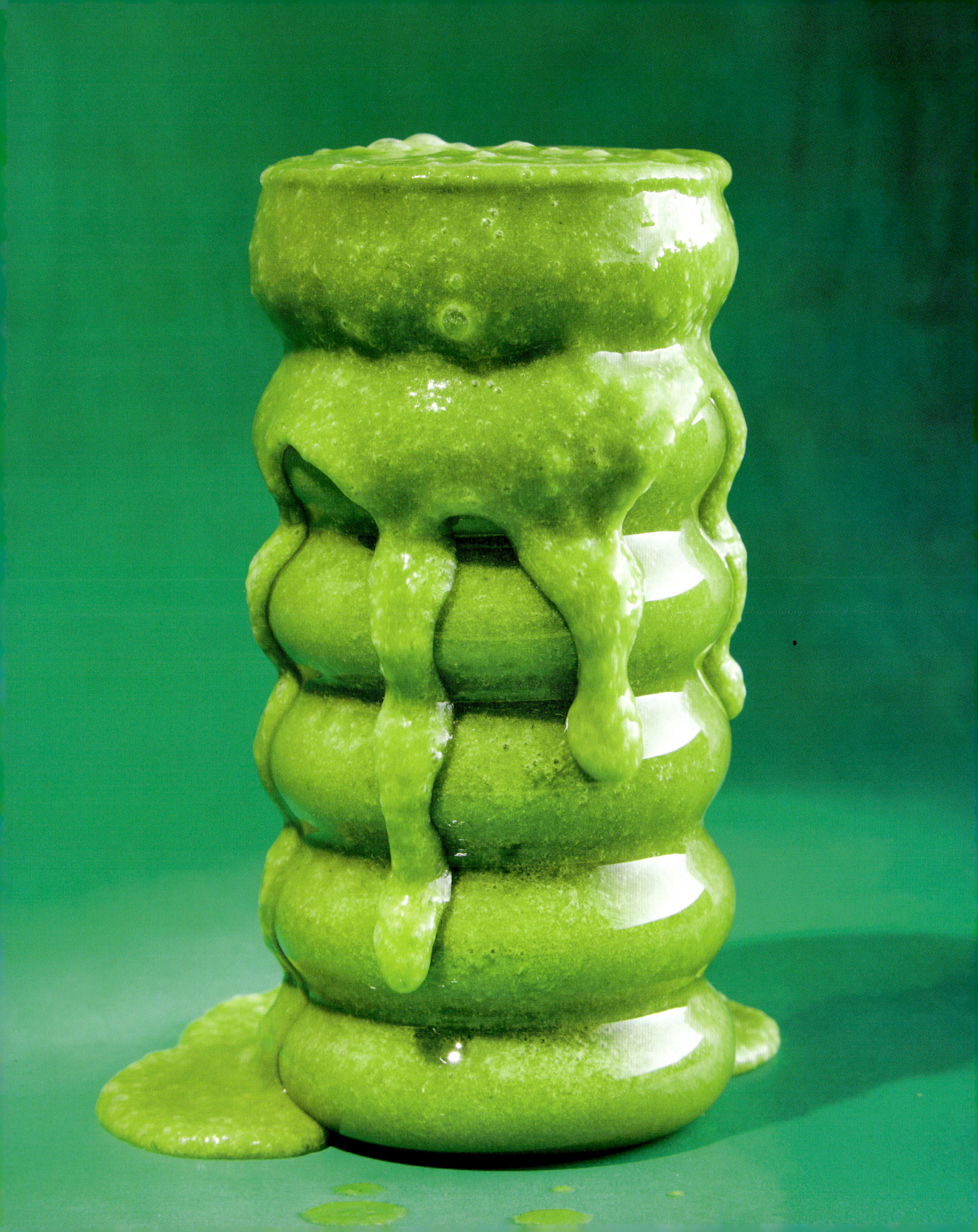

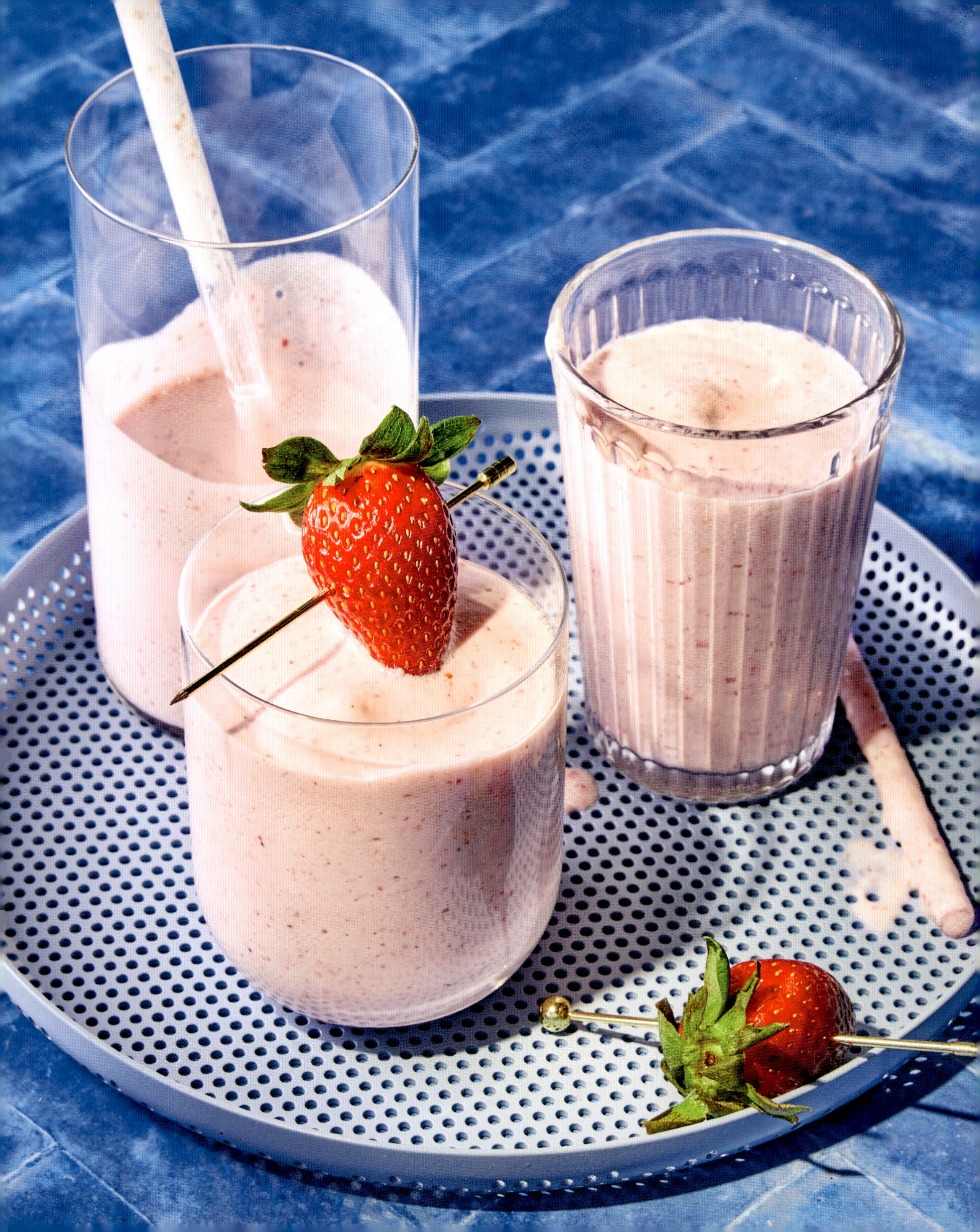

STONER-BERRY SHAKES

- ◆ **MAKES THREE 10½ OZ [320 ML] MILKSHAKES**
- ◆ **SERVING SIZE: 1 MILKSHAKE**
- ◆ **DOSAGE PER SERVING: FEELIN' GOOD (5 TO 6 MG THC); FOR SKY HIGH (10 TO 12 MG) USE 1 TSP CANNABIS GLYCERINE TINCTURE**
- ◆ **FOR VIRGIN (0 MG) SKIP CANNABIS GLYCERINE TINCTURE**

1 pt [480 g] strawberry ice cream, preferably Dr. Bombay Strawberry Cream Dream

1 lb [455 g] strawberries, hulled and quartered, plus 3 strawberries, hulled, to garnish

1 Tbsp light brown sugar

1 Tbsp fresh lemon juice

1 tsp vanilla extract

½ cup [120 ml] whole milk

½ tsp Cannabis Glycerine Tincture (page 15)

1. Remove the ice cream from the freezer to soften. In a small bowl, stir the strawberries, sugar, lemon juice, and vanilla together and let macerate for 20 minutes.

2. In a blender on high speed, blend the ice cream, macerated strawberry mixture, milk, and tincture until smooth and creamy. If using Dr. Bombay, you may have bits of cookie in your milkshake, which just makes it more delicious.

3. Pour into three glasses. Cut a slit in the bottom of each strawberry and hang a strawberry on the rim of each glass to serve.

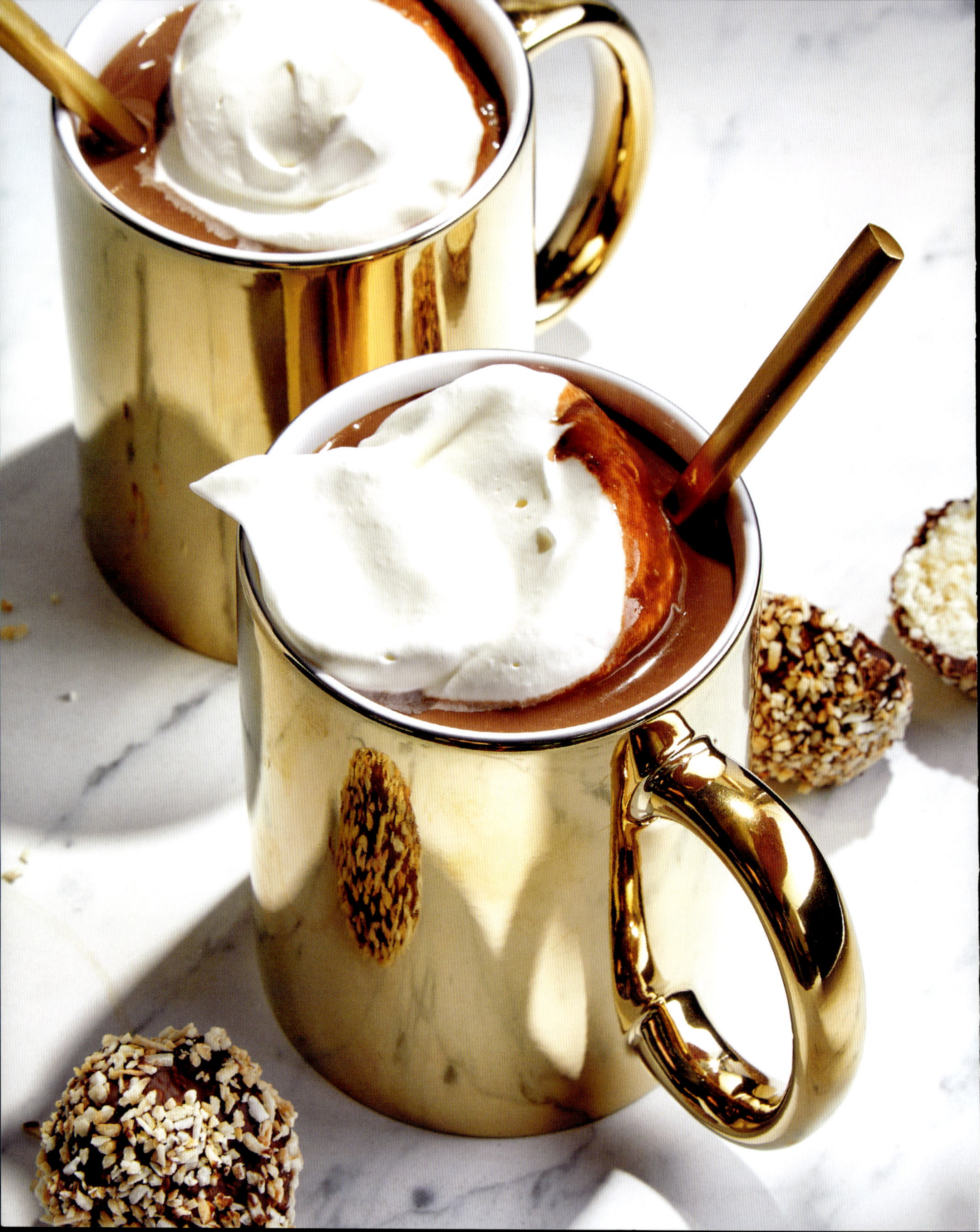

POT COCOA

- MAKES FIVE 1 CUP [240 ML] DRINKS
- SERVING SIZE: 1 DRINK
- DOSAGE PER SERVING: FEELIN' GOOD (5 TO 6 MG THC); FOR SKY HIGH (10 TO 12 MG) USE 2 TSP CANNABIS GLYCERINE TINCTURE
- FOR VIRGIN (0 MG) SKIP CANNABIS GLYCERINE TINCTURE

¾ cup [180 ml] heavy cream

5 cups [1.2 L] whole milk

6 Tbsp [90 g] packed light brown sugar

4 oz [115 g] unsweetened chocolate, chopped

3½ oz [100 g] bittersweet chocolate, chopped

⅛ tsp kosher salt

1 tsp Cannabis Glycerine Tincture (page 15)

½ tsp vanilla extract

1. In a tall jar using an immersion blender, whip the cream until stiff peaks form, about 3 minutes. Chill the whipped cream while you make the cocoa.

2. In a medium saucepan over medium heat, heat the milk until simmering. Lower the heat to low, add the sugar, both chocolates, and salt. Cook, stirring, until melted, 3 to 5 minutes. Remove from the heat, stir in the cannabis glycerine tincture, and vanilla, and divide among five mugs. Top each hot chocolate with some of the whipped cream.

HOT CANNABUTTERED RUM

- **MAKES TWELVE 9 FL OZ [270 ML] DRINKS**
- **SERVING SIZE: 1 DRINK**
- **DOSAGE PER SERVING: FEELIN' GOOD (5 TO 6 MG THC); FOR SKY HIGH (10 TO 12 MG) USE 4 TSP CANNABUTTER**
- **FOR VIRGIN (0 MG) SKIP CANNABUTTER**

FOR THE BATTER

½ cup [100 g] light brown sugar

½ cup [110 g] unsalted butter, at room temperature

2 tsp Cannabutter (page 15), at room temperature

1 tsp vanilla extract

1 tsp ground allspice

1 tsp ground cinnamon

1 tsp ground cloves

1 tsp ground nutmeg

⅛ tsp kosher salt

FOR THE DRINK

24 oz [720 ml] aged rum

Orange peels, for garnish

TO MAKE THE BATTER

1. In the bowl of a stand mixer fitted with the paddle attachment or pulsing in a food processor, beat the sugar, unsalted butter, cannabutter, vanilla, allspice, cinnamon, cloves, nutmeg, and salt until a smooth, thick batter forms. The batter will keep in an airtight container in the refrigerator for up to 5 days or in the freezer for 1 month.

TO MAKE THE DRINK

1. Add 2 Tbsp of the batter, 2 oz [60 ml] of the rum, and 6 oz [180 ml] of boiling water to a mug and stir to combine. Repeat with the remaining batter and rum.

2. For each drink, squeeze an orange peel over the top, rub it around the rim of the mug, and drop it in the drink.

HOT CANNABUTTERED RUM

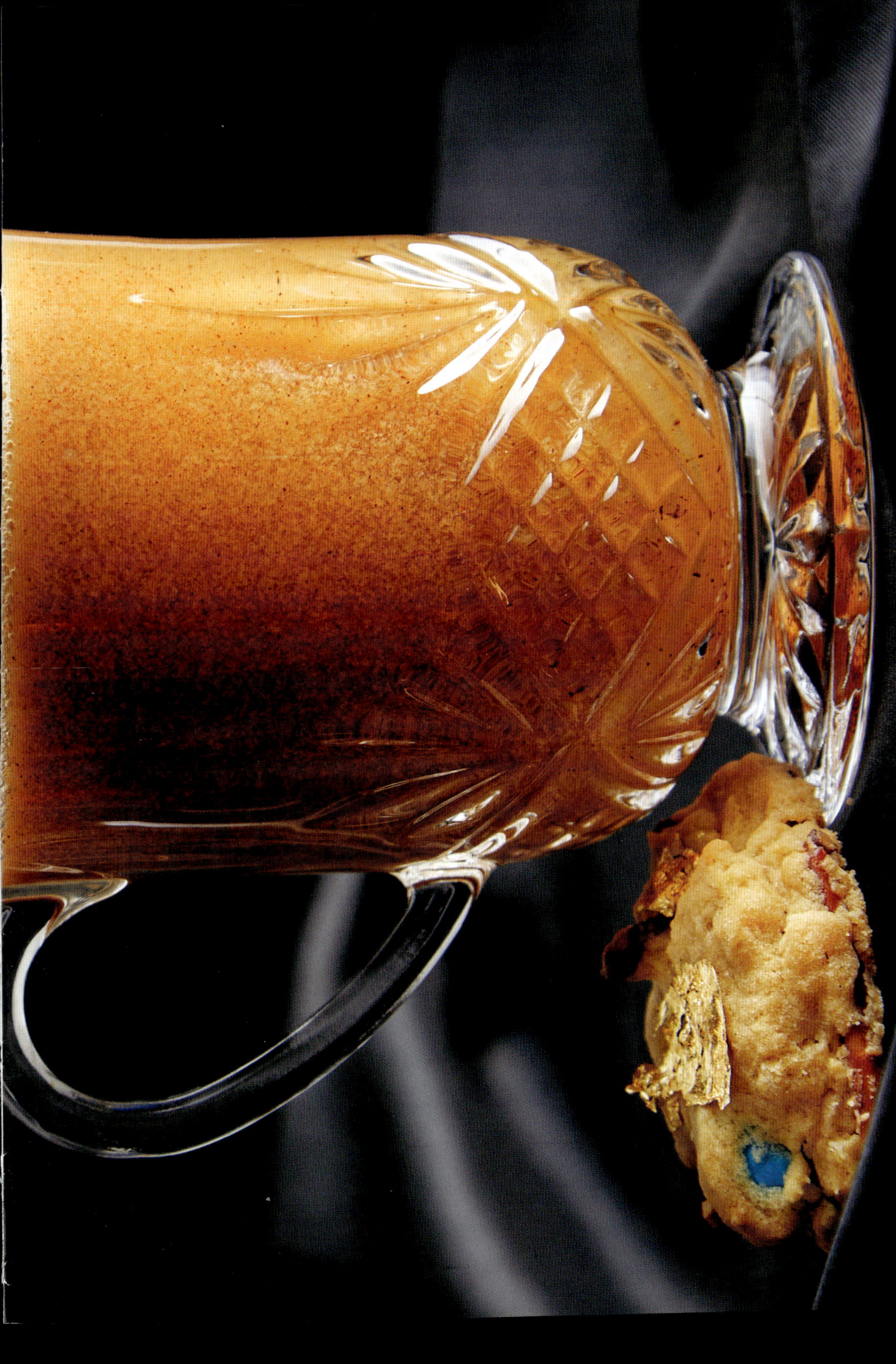

BLITZ SPRITZ

- MAKES ONE 6 FL OZ [180 ML] DRINK
- SERVING SIZE: 1 DRINK
- DOSAGE PER SERVING: FEELIN' GOOD (5 TO 6 MG THC); FOR SKY HIGH (10 TO 12 MG) USE ¼ TSP CANNABIS GRAIN-ALCOHOL TINCTURE
- FOR VIRGIN (0 MG) SKIP CANNABIS GRAIN-ALCOHOL TINCTURE

3 oz [90 ml] sparkling wine

2 oz [60 ml] Aperol

⅛ tsp or 12 drops Cannabis Grain-Alcohol Tincture (page 18)

1 oz [30 ml] soda water

Orange slice, for garnish

Fill a wineglass with ice, add the sparkling wine, Aperol, and tincture, and stir gently to combine. Top with the soda water and garnish with an orange slice.

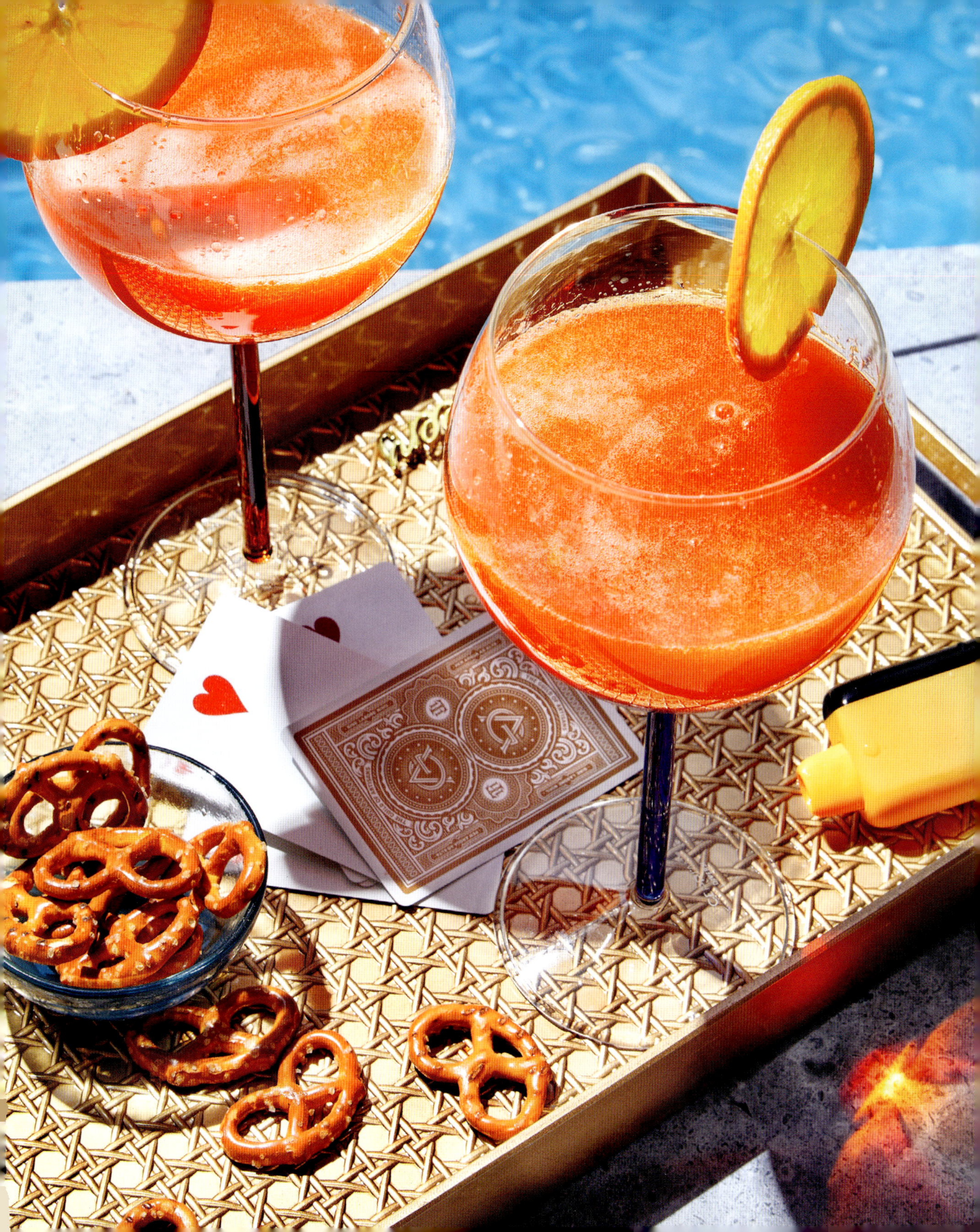

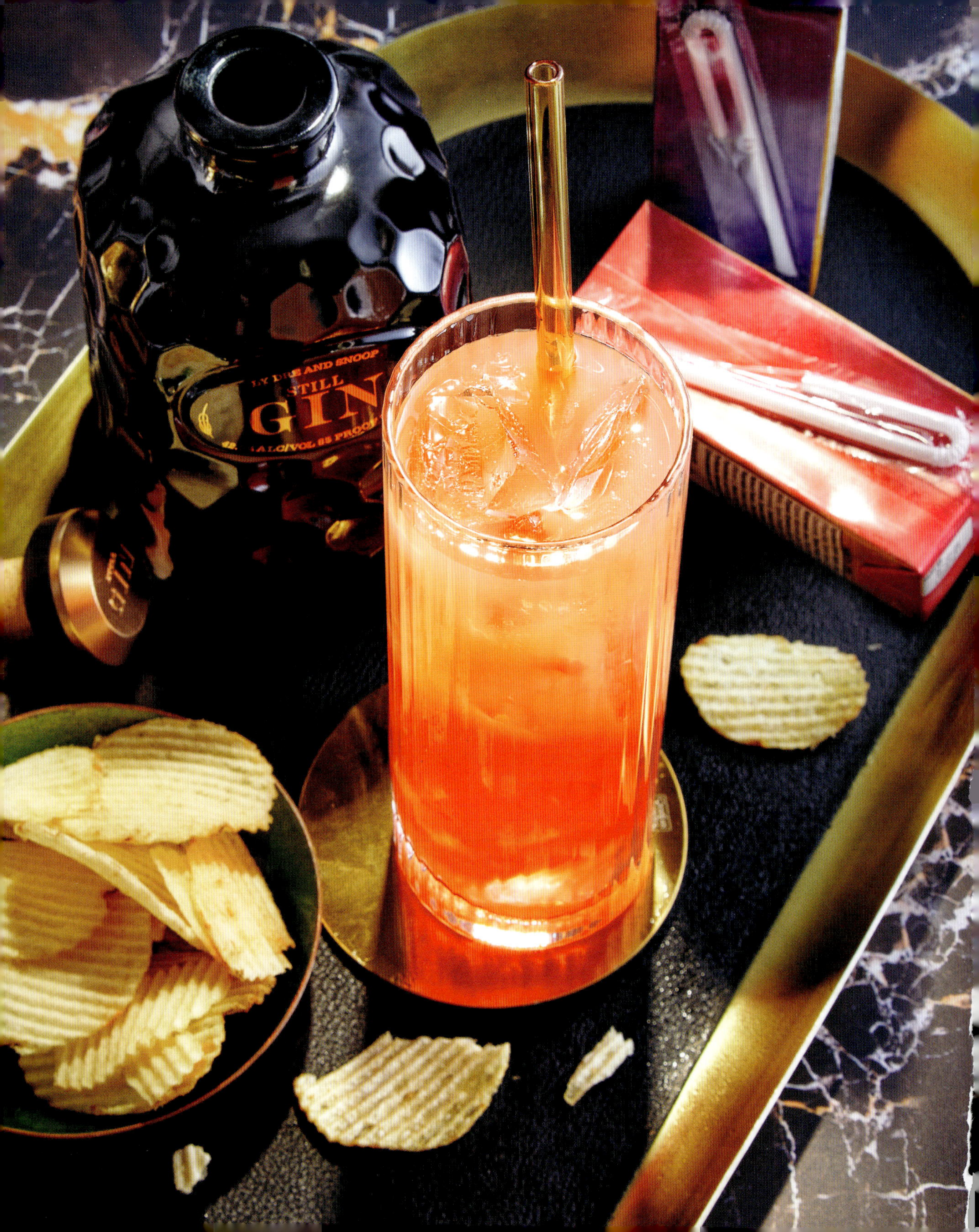
STILL
GIN

JACKED-UP GIN 'N' JUICE

- ◆ MAKES ONE 6 FL OZ [180 ML] DRINK
- ◆ SERVING SIZE: 1 DRINK
- ◆ DOSAGE PER SERVING: FEELIN' GOOD (5 TO 6 MG THC); FOR SKY HIGH (10 TO 12 MG) USE 20 DROPS CANNABIS GRAIN-ALCOHOL TINCTURE
- ◆ FOR VIRGIN (0 MG) SKIP CANNABIS GRAIN-ALCOHOL TINCTURE

1½ oz [45 ml] gin

10 drops Cannabis Grain-Alcohol Tincture (page 18)

4½ oz [135 ml] your favorite juice

In a highball glass, stir the gin and tincture together. Add ice to fill the glass. Top with the juice and stir to combine.

INDEX

A

Aperol
    Blitz Spritz, 166
apples
    Morning Glow Muffins, 107–8
Arnold Palmer in the Weeds, 152–53

B

Bacon Cheddar Scallion Biscuits, 120
baking tips, 10–11
bananas
    Tha Grass Smoovie, 156
    The New 'Naner Bread, 93–95
Bark, Peanut Butter Raisinet Pretzel, 136
bars
    Fruit Loops Bars with Benefits, 64
    PB, C, and J Bars, 67–68
Biscuits, Bacon Cheddar Scallion, 120
blackberries
    Four Berries and a Bud Fruit Pie, 96–97
Blitz Spritz, 166
Blondies, Loaded Brown-Butter, 60–61
blueberries
    Four Berries and a Bud Fruit Pie, 96–97
    Whole Weed Waffles with Blueberry Cannabis Compote, 114–16
bread
    Cannabis Corn Bread with Hot Honey Cannabutter, 117–18
    The New 'Naner Bread, 93–95
breakfast. *See* wake and bakes
brownies
    Dank Double-Chocolate Brownies, 55–56
    Peppermint Pot Brownies, 57–58
Bud-dermilk Pancakes with Stoner Syrup, 110–11
Burnt Lil Cheesecakes, 91–92
butter
    Cannabutter, 15
    Hot Honey Cannabutter, 117–18

C

cakes
    Burnt Lil Cheesecakes, 91–92
    Coconut Cannabis Cake, 87–88
    Ho-Ho Cupcakes with Cannabis Cream Filling, 75–76
    Mellow Yellow Cake, 80–81
    Morning Buzz Coffee Cake, 105–6
    Red Velvet Blundt Cake, 85–86
candies
    Marijuana Butter Mints, 127
    Mixed-Up Nut Toffee, 133
    Orange You High Yet Gummies, 124
    PB & THC Cups, 129
    Peanut Butter Raisinet Pretzel Bark, 136
    Toasted Coconut Cannabis Truffles, 130–32
cannabis
    baking with, 10–11
    Cannabis Corn Bread with Hot Honey Cannabutter, 117–18
    Cannabis Glycerine Tincture, 15
    Cannabis Grain-Alcohol Tincture, 18
    Cannabis Oil, 15
    Cannabutter, 15
    Decarbed Cannabis Flower, 14
Cannabutter, 15
    Cannabutter Crab Puffs, 147–48
    Hot Honey Cannabutter, 117–18
carrots
    Morning Glow Muffins, 107–8
cereal
    Fruit Loops Bars with Benefits, 64
    Snoopy Chow, 138
cheese
    Bacon Cheddar Scallion Biscuits, 120
    Burnt Lil Cheesecakes, 91–92
    Cannabutter Crab Puffs, 147–48
    Herb 'n' Cheese Fatties, 145–46
    Pourable Cream Cheese Frosting, 24
    Sugar Cookies Two Ways, 36–37
chocolate
    Chocolate Chip Cookies, 30–32
    Dank Double-Chocolate Brownies, 55–56
    Ho-Ho Cupcakes with Cannabis Cream Filling, 75–76

INDEX

Mixed-Up Nut Toffee, 133
The New 'Naner Bread, 93–95
PB & THC Cups, 129
Peppermint Pot Brownies, 57–58
Pot Cocoa, 161
Red Velvet Blundt Cake, 85–86
Snoopy Chow, 138
Super-Fudgy Frosting, 22
Toasted Coconut Cannabis Truffles, 130–32
coconut
    Coconut Cannabis Cake, 87–88
    Morning Glow Muffins, 107–8
    Toasted Coconut Cannabis Truffles, 130–32
Coffee Cake, Morning Buzz, 105–6
Connoisseur Cookies, 50
cookies
    Chocolate Chip Cookies, 30–32
    Connoisseur Cookies, 50
    Ganja Snaps, 43–45
    Nutter Butter Stoner Cookies, 46–47
    Oatmeal Raisin Cookies, 33–34
    Snooperdoodles, 40–42
    Sugar Cookies Two Ways, 36–37
corn
    Cannabis Corn Bread with Hot Honey Cannabutter, 117–18
    Hot Buttered Pot Corn, 141
Crab Puffs, Cannabutter, 147–48
cream cheese
    Burnt Lil Cheesecakes, 91–92
    Cannabutter Crab Puffs, 147–48
    Pourable Cream Cheese Frosting, 24
    Sugar Cookies Two Ways, 36–37
Cupcakes, Ho-Ho, with Cannabis Cream Filling, 75–76

D

Dank Double-Chocolate Brownies, 55–56
dates
    Morning Glow Muffins, 107–8
Decarbed Cannabis Flower, 14
drinks
    Arnold Palmer in the Weeds, 152–53
    Blitz Spritz, 166
    Tha Grass Smoovie, 156
    Hot Cannabuttered Rum, 162–63
    Jacked-Up Gin 'n' Juice, 169
    Pot Cocoa, 161
    Stoner-berry Shakes, 159

F

Four Berries and a Bud Fruit Pie, 96–97
frostings
    Pourable Cream Cheese Frosting, 24
    Super-Fudgy Frosting, 22
    Vanilla Buttercream Frosting, 20
Fruit Loops Bars with Benefits, 64

G

Ganja Snaps, 43–45
Gin 'n' Juice, Jacked-Up, 169
Glaze, Lemon, 26
Glycerine Tincture, Cannabis, 15
Grain-Alcohol Tincture, Cannabis, 18
Tha Grass Smoovie, 156
Gummies, Orange You High Yet, 124

H

Herb 'n' Cheese Fatties, 145–46
Ho-Ho Cupcakes with Cannabis Cream Filling, 75–76
Hot Buttered Pot Corn, 141
Hot Cannabuttered Rum, 162–63
hot dogs
    Pigs in a Grass Blanket, 142

I

ice cream
    Stoner-berry Shakes, 159

J

Jacked-Up Gin 'n' Juice, 169
jam
    PB, C, and J Bars, 67–68

L

lemons
    Arnold Palmer in the Weeds, 152–53
    Lemon Glaze, 26
    Lemon Poppy Seed Pot Muffins, 72–74
Loaded Brown-Butter Blondies, 60–61

M

macadamia nuts
    Loaded Brown-Butter Blondies, 60–61
M&Ms
    Connoisseur Cookies, 50
maple syrup
    Stoner Syrup, 110–11
Marijuana Butter Mints, 127
marshmallows and marshmallow fluff
    Fruit Loops Bars with Benefits, 64
    Ho-Ho Cupcakes with Cannabis Cream Filling, 75–76
Mary Jane Pudding, 101
Mellow Yellow Cake, 80–81
Mints, Marijuana Butter, 127
Mixed-Up Nut Toffee, 133
Morning Buzz Coffee Cake, 105–6
Morning Glow Muffins, 107–8
muffins
    Lemon Poppy Seed Pot Muffins, 72–74
    Morning Glow Muffins, 107–8
    Pumpkin Pot Muffins, 69–70

N

The New 'Naner Bread, 93–95
nuts. *See also individual nuts*
    Mixed-Up Nut Toffee, 133
    Nutter Butter Stoner Cookies, 46–47

O

Oatmeal Raisin Cookies, 33–34
Oil, Cannabis, 15
oranges
    Tha Grass Smoovie, 156
    Orange You High Yet Gummies, 124

P

Pancakes, Bud-dermilk, with Stoner Syrup, 110–11
peanut butter
    Nutter Butter Stoner Cookies, 46–47
    PB & THC Cups, 129
    PB, C, and J Bars, 67–68
    Peanut Butter Raisinet Pretzel Bark, 136
    Snoopy Chow, 138
peanuts
    Mary Jane Pudding, 101
    PB, C, and J Bars, 67–68
pecans
    Morning Glow Muffins, 107–8
    Oatmeal Raisin Cookies, 33–34
Peppermint Pot Brownies, 57–58
Pie, Four Berries and a Bud Fruit, 96–97
Pigs in a Grass Blanket, 142
pineapple
    Loaded Brown-Butter Blondies, 60–61
    Morning Glow Muffins, 107–8
popcorn
    Hot Buttered Pot Corn, 141
potato chips
    Connoisseur Cookies, 50
Pot Cocoa, 161
Pourable Cream Cheese Frosting, 24
pretzels
    Connoisseur Cookies, 50
    Peanut Butter Raisinet Pretzel Bark, 136
Pudding, Mary Jane, 101
puff pastry

Cannabutter Crab Puffs, 147–48
Pumpkin Pot Muffins, 69–70

R

raisins
    Morning Glow Muffins, 107–8
    Oatmeal Raisin Cookies, 33–34
    Peanut Butter Raisinet Pretzel Bark, 136
raspberries
    Four Berries and a Bud Fruit Pie, 96–97
Red Velvet Blundt Cake, 85–86
Rum, Hot Cannabuttered, 162–63

S

Shakes, Stoner-berry, 159
smoothie
    Tha Grass Smoovie, 156
Snooperdoodles, 40–42
Snoopy Chow, 138
spinach
    Tha Grass Smoovie, 156
Stoner-berry Shakes, 159
Stoner Syrup, 110–11
strawberries
    Four Berries and a Bud Fruit Pie, 96–97
    Stoner-berry Shakes, 159
Sugar Cookies Two Ways, 36–37
Super-Fudgy Frosting, 22

T

tea
    Arnold Palmer in the Weeds, 152–53
Toasted Coconut Cannabis Truffles, 130–32
Toffee, Mixed-Up Nut, 133
Truffles, Toasted Coconut Cannabis, 130–32

V

Vanilla Buttercream Frosting, 20

W

Waffles, Whole Weed, with Blueberry Cannabis
    Compote, 114–16
wake and bakes
    Bacon Cheddar Scallion Biscuits, 120
    Bud-dermilk Pancakes with Stoner Syrup, 110–11
    Cannabis Corn Bread with Hot Honey Cannabutter, 117–18
    Morning Buzz Coffee Cake, 105–6
    Morning Glow Muffins, 107–8
    Whole Weed Waffles with Blueberry Cannabis Compote, 114–16
walnuts
    Chocolate Chip Cookies, 30–32
    Dank Double-Chocolate Brownies, 55–56
white chocolate
    Fruit Loops Bars with Benefits, 64
    Loaded Brown-Butter Blondies, 60–61
    Peanut Butter Raisinet Pretzel Bark, 136
Whole Weed Waffles with Blueberry Cannabis
    Compote, 114–16
wine
    Blitz Spritz, 166

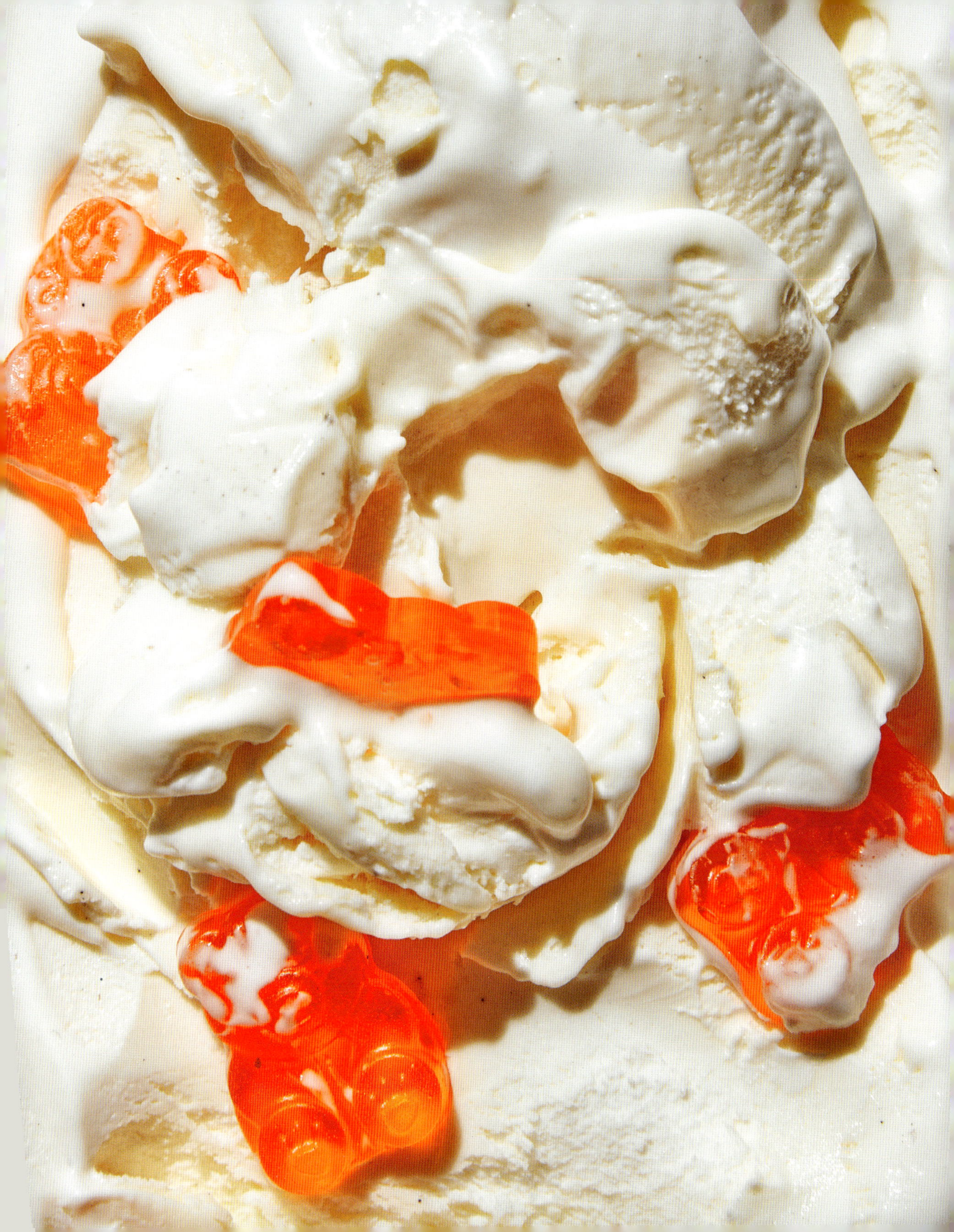

Text copyright © 2025 by **DEATH ROW.**

Photographs copyright © 2025 by **ANTONIS ACHILLEOS.**

All rights reserved. No part of this book may be reproduced in any form without written permission from the publisher.

Library of Congress Cataloging-in-Publication Data available.

ISBN 978-1-7972-1761-1

Manufactured in China.

Prop styling by **ED GALLAGHER.**
Food styling by **VICTORIA GRANOF.**
Design by **VANESSA DINA.**
Typesetting by **BROOKE JOHNSON.**

Editorial direction, writing, recipe development and testing, and weed knowledge: **BETSY ANDREWS, SARAH BILLINGSLEY, TORRE BLAKE, TIFFANY CHIN, JESSICA LING, SEAN SORRELL, SARA RAMAKER, KELSEY WONG.**

10 9 8 7 6 5 4 3 2 1

Chronicle books and gifts are available at special quantity discounts to corporations, professional associations, literacy programs, and other organizations. For details and discount information, please contact our premiums department at corporatesales@chroniclebooks.com or at 1-800-759-0190.

Chronicle Books LLC
680 Second Street
San Francisco, California 94107
www.chroniclebooks.com